Newham London

5/11/10		
08 APR 2011		
27 APR 2011		
01 SEP 2011		
12 FEB 2012		

24 hour automated telephone renewal line
0115 929 3388
Or online at www.newham.gov.uk

LSQ0018h(2.10.03)

**This book must be returned (or its issue renewed)
on or before the date stamped above**

Understanding
Guru Granth Sahib
The Living Guru

Understanding
Guru Granth Sahib
The Living Guru

Satjit Wadva

Introduction by

Air Commodore **Jasjit Singh** AVSM, VrC, VM (Retd)

KW Publishers Pvt Ltd
New Delhi

KW Publishers Pvt Ltd

NEW DELHI: 4676/21, First Floor, Ansari Road, Daryaganj, New Delhi 110002
E mail@kwpub.in/knowledgeworld@vsnl.net T +91.11.23263498 / 43528107
MUMBAI: 15 Jay Kay Industrial Estate, Linking Road Extn., Santacruz (W), Mumbai 400054
E mumbai@kwpub.in T +91.22.26614110 / 26613505
w w w . k w p u b . i n

ISBN 13: 978-93-80502-34-2

Published by Kalpana Shukla, KW Publishers Pvt Ltd
4676/21, First Floor, Ansari Road, Daryaganj, New Delhi 110002

Printed at Aegean Offset Printers, Greater Noida (U.P)

Contents

Introduction

.... I have studied the scriptures of the great religions, but I do not find elsewhere the same power of appeal to the heart and mind as I find here in these volumes (English translation of *Siri Guru Granth Sahib*). They are compact in spite of their length, and are a revelation of the vast reach of the human heart, varying from the most noble concept of God, to the recognition and indeed the insistence upon the practical needs of the human body. There is something strangely modern about these scriptures and this puzzled me until I learned that they are in fact comparatively modern, compiled as late as the 16th century, when explorers were beginning to discover that the globe upon which we all live is a single entity divided only by arbitrary lines of our own making. Perhaps this sense of unity is the source of power I find in these volumes. **They speak to a person of any religion or of none.** They speak for the human heart and the searching mind. ...

— Pearl S. Buck, Nobel Laureate[1]

The *Guru Granth Sahib* or *Adi Granth*, is the holy Granth (*holy book*) and the final Guru of the Sikhs which is more than just a scripture of the Sikhs and contains the actual words spoken by the founding Gurus of the Sikh religion besides the words and teachings of various saints from other religions especially Hinduism and Islam. Guru Gobind Singh

---

1. From the foreword to the English translation of *Sri Guru Granth Sahib* by Dr. Gopal Singh, 1960.

(1666–1708), the tenth of the Sikh Gurus, affirmed the sacred text *Adi Granth* as his successor, terminating the line of human Gurus, and elevating the text to *Guru Granth Sahib*. In the last stages of his mortal life Guru Gobind Singh said that the Sikhs were to treat the Granth Sahib as their next Guru. Guru Ji said: *"Sab Sikhan ko hukam hai Guru Manyo Granth"* meaning "All Sikhs are commanded to acknowledge the Granth as their Guru."

Since then its text has remained the holy scripture of the Sikhs, worshipped as the living embodiment of the Ten Gurus. The role of *Guru Granth Sahib*, as a source or guide of prayer, is pivotal in worship in Sikhism.

To understand and appreciate the true meaning, value and teachings of *Guru Granth Sahib*, one must turn to the beginning of the Sikh religion and the first and greatest of all gurus, Guru Nanak (1469-1539). The doctrine that he taught, through parables, verses and hymns in the spoken language of the period and region of Punjab extending as it did at that time from the Khyber Pass to the River Yamuna in the east essentially was a doctrine of salvation through the divine Name. For Guru Nanak, as it was for other saints like Kabir, salvation was to be found in mystical union with God. But the essential difference in Guru Nanak's teachings is his explanation of the path to salvation in consistent terms to the goal of ultimate experience providing originality in the coherence and the compelling beauty of his teachings. One central assumption deals with the nature of God, the One, who is without form (*nirankar*), eternal (*akal*), indefinable (*alakh*). At the same time Guru Nanak's teachings also make some assumptions about the nature of Man, who by nature is wilfully blind to the divine revelations around him, seeking salvation through various other means which represent the ultimate unreality (*maya*) of the values which it represents.

Siri Guru Granth Sahib is a voluminous text of 1430 *angs* (pages), compiled and composed during the period of Sikh Gurus, from 1469 to 1708. It is a collection of hymns or *shabad*, which describe the qualities of God and why one should meditate on God's name. The *Adi Granth* was first compiled by the fifth Sikh guru, Guru Arjan Dev (1563–1606), from hymns of the first five Sikh gurus and other great saints, including those of the Hindu and Muslim faith. After the demise of the tenth Sikh guru many handwritten copies were prepared for distribution by Baba Deep Singh. Written in the Gurmukhi script, predominantly in archaic Punjabi with occasional use of other languages including Braj, Punjabi, Khariboli (Hindi), Sanskrit, regional dialects, and Persian, often coalesced under the generic title of Sant Bhasha.

Sikhs consider the *Siri Guru Granth Sahib* a spiritual guide for all mankind for all generations to come, and it plays a central role in guiding the Sikhs' way of life. Its place in Sikh devotional life is based on two fundamental principles; that the text is divine revelation, and that all answers regarding religion and morality can be discovered within it. Its hymns and teachings are called *Gurbani* or "Word of the guru" and sometimes *Dhur ki bani* or "Word of God". Thus, in Sikh theology, the revealed divine word is the Guru.

The numerous holy men other than the Sikh Gurus whose writing were included in the *Siri Guru Granth Sahib* are collectively referred to as Bhagats "devotees" and their writings are referred to as *Bhagat bani* "Word of Devotees". These saints belonged to different social and religious backgrounds, including Hindus and Muslims, cobblers and untouchables. Though *Sri Guru Granth Sahib Ji* contains the compositions of both Sikh Gurus as well the other great saints (Bhagats) — including those of the Hindu and Muslim faith — no distinction whatsoever is made between the works of Sikh Gurus and the works of the Bhagats contained within the *Siri Guru Granth*

Sahib. But the titles "Guru" and "Bhagat" should not be misleading. The *Guru Granth Sahib* is the sole and final successor of the line of gurus in the Sikh religion. Anyone claiming the status of living guru is considered a heretic.

Guru Granth Sahib is an encyclopaedia in song. It is a compendium of philosophy in verse, a treasury of the music of saints. *Gurbani* has descended from the divine and was received by mystics who put it in the form of of Word (*shabad*). It charts the pathways to the mountain peak of highest realisation. It is a guide to social reformation, a clarion call to equality of all classes, races, and religions — long before the word 'secular' came into vogue. It is a coffer containing secrets of yogis, Sufis, saints of all paths and ages—locked to the blind, open to hearts filled with devotion. *Adi Granth*, the First Book, not in chronological time but because it is a vehicle of the First Truths that dawn when the supplicant approaches the throne of the Timeless Person, *Akal Purukh*, and 'by His Grace' all one's exterior openings close, 'one's self is beautified, the light shines, and all the lotuses of consciousness come into full bloom.'

The voices of thirty-six saints and servants of God sing the nearly six thousand songs as though a single choir in the cathedral of the universal mind. Spanning more than four centuries of exterior crises and simultaneously interior revelations, they all agree not only in their themes but even in words which have become a guiding beacon to people of different faiths and position in life and society for more than three centuries. Though they spoke languages as diverse as the Sanskrit of Jayadeva and Persian of Baba Farid, by some magic of the mystical unity of minds the languages merge and become just the Word (*shabad*), the sacred speech (*bani*).

In the rush and humdrum of modern life we often fail to absorb the true meaning of the Holy Granth even when we read the text. This may make someone appear religious even to himself, but the teachings of the Gurus require all human beings to be god fearing and respect life and its dignity. Satjit Wadva has done humanity a great service by trying to help the reader, young or old, rich or poor, understand the real meaning and intent of *Siri Guru Granth Sahib* so that they can enrich their lives from the teachings of the Gurus.

Jasjit Singh
Air Commodore (Retd)

The Living Guru

The Guru Granth Sahib is the living Guru of the Sikhs. It is the embodiment of the spirit of all the ten Gurus who came in human form. The Gurbani, the religious poetry of the Guru Granth Sahib covers the entire spectrum of life. It shows the devotee how to live life meaningfully so that the purpose of life is achieved. On the physical level, it tells you how to conduct your behaviour in society; at the mental level, it helps you understand the profound truths of life in amazingly simple words; at the emotional level, it fills your heart with love for the divine so that you remain attuned to the Creator all the time. The Guru Granth Sahib discusses mundane matters, on the one hand and, on the other, touches the peaks of mysticism and spiritualism just as easily and effortlessly.

The Guru Granth Sahib is your guide, friend and philosopher. You can feel the presence of the divine spark in you in the presence of the Guru Granth Sahib. You can get answers to your questions from the Guru Granth Sahib. You can gain an understanding of life by simply reading and listening to the Gurbani. The Guru Granth Sahib is the Guru that cares for you, holds you by the hand and leads you to your goal, and makes your life comfortable in this world as well as the other world. Thus, in every sense of the word and at various levels of consciousness, the Guru Granth Sahib is the living Guru.

Guru Nanak passed on the spark of divine light to Bhai Lehna and made him Guru Angad, a part of himself. The tradition was kept alive by the subsequent Gurus. Guru Gobind Singh, the tenth Guru of the Sikhs, declared that after him the Guru would not appear in the human form. He said that from then onwards, the Guru Granth Sahib would be their Guru.

'*Sab Sikhan ko hukam hai guru manyo Granth*,' he said. All the Sikhs are instructed to follow the Granth as their Guru. '*Guru Granth ji manyo pargat guran ki deh*,' he continued to explain that the Guru Granth is the culmination of the teachings of all the Gurus. In other words, he made it clear that the Guru Granth Sahib was the embodiment of the all the ten Gurus preceding it.

In the Guru Granth Sahib, they would be able to see their Gurus who had come in the human form. In the Guru Granth Sahib, they would find answers to their questions that may rise on their spiritual or worldly path. And, in the Guru Granth Sahib, they will find the spirit of their Guru that will help them surrender themselves completely to the divine power.

The Guru Granth Sahib encompasses all the qualities that each Guru individually and all the Gurus collectively professed and practised.

The first Guru, Guru Nanak, received the divine light and laid the foundation of the concept of the ideal man. He made a sketch of what that person should be.

The second Guru, Guru Angad, filled it with devotion, discipleship and surrender. He taught the real meaning of being a Sikh, a disciple, a shishya.

The third Guru, Guru Amardas, initiated the tradition of sharing and forgiveness. He started the tradition of langar where everyone would sit together and eat the food cooked in the common kitchen.

The fourth Guru, Guru Ramdas, brought in service of the poor, the suffering and the needy. He created a place where this service could be provided. He asked a Muslim to lay the foundation of the Harmandir Sahib, thereby emphasising that he made no distinction on the basis of religion.

The fifth Guru, Guru Arjan, brought in the virtues of compassion, self-sacrifice and total acceptance of the Divine Will. His contributions to the Guru Granth Sahib are the maximum.

The sixth Guru, Guru Hargobind, introduced valour and courage. Known as Miri Piri de Malik, he struck a balance between the practical and spiritual aspects of life.

The seventh Guru, Guru Har Rai, strengthened the tradition of langar, sadh sangat and spread the word of Guru Nanak by sending missionaries far and wide.

The eighth Guru, Guru Harkrishan, the child Guru, provided the healing touch to the suffering people.

The ninth Guru, Guru Tegh Bahadur, broke all boundaries between people on the basis of caste or religion. He sacrificed his life for the faith of others thereby setting an unparalleled example of selfless sacrifice in the world. His contributions to the Guru Granth Sahib were added by his son and the tenth master, Guru Gobind Singh, who was a perfect example of humility; he did not include his own poetic compositions in the Guru Granth Sahib.

The tenth Guru, Guru Gobind Singh, gave a practical shape to the followers of Guru Nanak. He baptised them formally and bestowed his own form and spirit on them. He instilled courage in them so that they would not be passive spectators only but take up arms against injustice. He created a tribe of saint-soldiers who would fight for justice and against oppression against anyone.

The Guru Granth Sahib records all these qualities. While it teaches you to live peacefully, it also inspires you to do or die in the battlefield. While it instructs you to live your life in remembrance of God, day and night, all the time and with every breath, it also tells you to work hard and earn your living so that you do not become a burden on the society. All in all, it instructs you to look within and concentrate on self-improvement rather than preaching to others.

The concept of Guru is of utmost importance in Sikhism. Man, in his present state, cannot find true knowledge without the Guru. Even at the mundane level, we are incapable of teaching ourselves; we need teachers and schools and colleges to learn the basic skills and information that can help us adjust in the society. Therefore, it is not surprising that we cannot attain true knowledge without the Guru.

Guru Nanak says in Asa-di-Var:

Je sau chanda ugvey suraj charhey hajaar,
Etey chanan hondeaan Guru bin ghor andhaar,

It means that even if there were a hundred moons and a thousand suns, without the Guru it would be pitch dark. Of course, he means the darkness of ignorance. Just as darkness is the absence of light, ignorance is the absence of knowledge. True knowledge is very different from what is commonly known as knowledge. In fact, we often mistake information to be knowledge. Information can be collected from umpteen sources — books, people, environment, television, radio and now almost everything you want to know can be known from the Internet.

But the one and only source of true knowledge is the Guru. How does the Guru impart such knowledge? The Guru is not just a teacher; he is much more. He creates the atmosphere around him that makes learning possible. It is the brilliance of his knowledge that creates the light around him and whoever comes close to him is blessed with it. Imagine a dark room in which light falls only through a small hole in the roof. If you remain out of the direct path of the ray of light, you will remain in darkness. But the moment you come under the ray of light, you are bathed in light and you, too, start glowing in the radiance.

What is true knowledge? We have already said that knowledge is different from information. Knowledge is also not scholarship. You may be a great scientist, a philosopher or an engineer yet you may be quite ignorant about life. Life is very vast and your area of excellence is limited. Indeed, most intellectuals miss true knowledge because they focus all their energy on a small sphere of knowledge. This is the age of specialisation, which means knowing more and more about less and less.

In a nursery class, a teacher was being very innovative when teaching the concept of blindness to three-year-olds. She told them the story of the elephant and the blind men who touched one portion of the elephant and declared what it was. The man who felt his ear said it was a fan; the man who touched his legs said it was a pole; the man who felt his trunk said that it was a snake, and so on. She told them the whole story without giving them the word blind. She wanted them to figure out the answer on their own. So, after telling the whole story, she asked, "Who were these men?" A smart young child promptly replied, "Specialists!"

True knowledge means 'knowing through experience.' Let me give you an example. When I talk about an apple, you get the taste of the apple in your mouth and you immediately understand what I am talking about. But for a child who has never tasted an apple, it would be very difficult to know exactly what an apple is. At best, he will understand the shape of the apple; he will feel the apple and know its texture; he will smell it and know its flavour, but he will not know its taste until he has eaten it and relished it.

Now, the experience of true knowledge is not as common as apples; in fact, it is extremely rare. The Gurbani says that experience of true knowledge is like *gunge ki mithai.* When a dumb person eats a sweet, he knows the taste in his mouth but has no means of expressing it because he cannot speak. The divine experience is somewhat like that; you know it, you can feel it, but cannot express it because you have no words to express it. Even if you coined new words to express it, no one will understand you because they have never had the same experience— they have never 'tasted' it. Thus, only the Guru will understand you because only the Guru can help you experience it in the first place.

The Guru Granth Sahib contains the collective knowledge of not only the Sikh Gurus but of many other saints and sages who had arrived at the same truths through their personal experience. It is remarkable that Guru Arjan Dev ji, who first compiled the Guru Granth Sahib, included the writings of the Gurus and the Bhagats, regardless of their religious or social background. Truth is not the monopoly of the rich and the learned; indeed, often the illiterate and the poor are far ahead in knowing the truth. Similarly, knowledge is also not the prerogative of the old and elderly; sometimes, the young can understand profound truths more easily because they are innocent and their minds are not covered with the dust of time.

The Guru Granth Sahib is unique in having compositions of sage-poets and mystics of different faiths, including those of Kabir, Baba Farid, Namdev, Jaidev, Dhanna Bhagat and Ravidas. Guru Gobind Singh, the tenth Guru, later enshrined the Holy Book as the eleventh Guru, a living testament to the *bani* or sayings of the Gurus.

Meticulously compiled and arranged into 5,894 hymns, the Adi Granth is set equally meticulously to 31 ragas of the classical music tradition, which has a powerful appeal to the heart as much as the mind.

This setting to music forms the underlying basis of the classification of hymns into Ashtapadas or hymns of eight verses, Chhands or verses of six lines, Chaupadas or hymns of four verses. The Guru Granth Sahib is intricately divided according to ragas, the metre of the poem, the author of the poem and its ghar in which the raga is to be sung. It has a fascinating raga-mala towards the end of the Holy Text, which is an index of musical measures.

Thus, the Guru Granth Sahib is the fountainhead of knowledge, expressed in poetry and set to music. It is rightly described as 'musicalisation of thought.' Like a spring, it bursts forth and flows down the mountains and plains in all its glory. Like a river, it allows all the streams and rivulets to join in and flow on. And like a river, it is always flowing, always new and always the same. Not that the words change in Guru Granth Sahib but the meaning changes for the seeker as he moves on the path of understanding. The Guru Granth Sahib is the living Guru as it helps you walk on the path that leads to true knowledge; it lights up the path for you so that you are aware of the dangers on the way; it helps you cross the barriers by throwing light on the path; and it guides you to the ultimate goal.

The Guru is not a subject of sight but a subject of sound. The Guru has to be heard, not seen. And, the Guru Granth Sahib is the talking Guru. The significance of the Guru Granth Sahib lies in its articulation. No wonder, kirtan and recitation are given so much importance. Kirtan is singing the Gurbani tunefully, melodiously. Music has a way of piercing your heart like nothing else. And, when the Gurbani is sung, you cannot remain untouched, no matter how rigid you are, regardless of whether you understand the language or not. Rabindranath Tagore did not understand the Gurmukhi language but he used to sit for hours in the Golden Temple listening to kirtan. He said music is universal and is not dependent on language. It is felt and understood not only by human beings but by animals and plants as well.

The historical gurudwaras have maintained the tradition of uninterrupted kirtan throughout the day. You can go in at any time and listen to the Guru's bani being sung melodiously, and feel blessed. It is like the flowing river. All you need to do is bend down, make a cup of your hands and take a drink of the water. The living Guru is there for you, overflowing with the sound; all you need to do is to take your pitcher and fill it with pure bliss.

Editing of the Guru Granth Sahib

Guru Nanak was born in 1469. This was the time when the Bhakti Movement in India was at its peak. Bhakti means personal devotion to God. The Bhakti Movement started in South India between the 7th and 12th centuries with saints like Shankara, Ramanuja and Madhwa. Later, in the 14th and 15th centuries, it gained momentum in North India due to the Muslim conquests. The saints of the Bhakti Movement were men and women of humble origin like Guru Nanak, Ramanand, Kabir, Namdev, Surdas and others. They came from all castes and classes. They went from place to place, singing devotional songs and creating awareness among people that there is one God and that service of humanity is the best form of worship and all men are equal.

There was spirituality in the air. Other than the saints who composed beautiful verses, even the common men rode high on the wave of spirituality that engulfed them. The language they used was the common dialect spoken by the common illiterate poor men and women. But they spoke a language that was poetic and they set it to music, and sang their songs. No wonder then that most of these verses were not written down. They were passed down from generation to generation, just like folk songs and folklore.

"At the time of Guru Nanak, Punjab had no set language. There were different dialects and scripts like Sharda, Takri, Persian and Bhatt Akhri.

The 52-letter script was a mixture of several languages. Guru Nanak deleted the superfluous letters and composed Patti of 35 letters only. Then he asked Bhai Lehna to put all the letters in a proper order. Bhai Lehna was a scholar and a poet, and he knew all these scripts. So Guru Angad Dev ji was the first to come up with the script he called Gurmukhi since it had been pronounced by his Guru. Gradually, this script was adopted by the people of Punjab and came to be known as Punjabi." (Dr Trilochan Singh, *Jeevan Charitar – Guru Nanak Dev*, 395).

By the time the fifth master Guru Arjan Dev ji started composing his shabads, he realised that there were hundreds of hymns of his predecessors that needed to be recorded properly. Therefore, he decided to compile them in one book.

It was a daunting task to put together all the bani, written or unwritten, under one cover. Only an enlightened master could have sifted the genuine from the fake verses. During the process of collecting the bani, he included the bani of many of the Hindu saints and Sufi sages of the Bhakti Movement. He included the bani of the saints and Bhatts irrespective of their caste, colour, creed or religion.

Then he decided on the format of the book and started the work in earnest. He dictated the bani to four writers — Sant Dass, Haria, Sukha and Mansa Ram. (Dr Gursharan Kaur Jaggi, *Guru Arjan Dev*, p. 16). The entire work of writing the Granth was given to Bhai Gurdass. The compilation was completed in 1604 AD and it was enshrined in the Harmandir Sahib, Amritsar, by none other than Baba Buddha ji who had conferred Guruship on Guru Angad Dev ji, Guru Amardas ji, Guru Ramdas ji, Guru Arjan Dev ji, and later on, Guru Hargobind ji as well.

Although it was the tenth master, Guru Gobind Singh ji who formally declared the Guru Granth Sahib to be the Guru of the Sikhs, Guru Arjan Dev ji had so much reverence for this Adi Granth that after its compilation, he seated it on an elevated position and slept on the floor by its side. He said: *Pothi parmeshwar ka thaan.*

Contents of the Guru Granth Sahib

The Gurbani in the Guru Granth Sahib is arranged according to the ragas. Under each raga, the bani of Guru Nanak comes first as Mahalla 1, and then the bani of Guru Angad Dev as Mahalla 2, followed by Guru Amardas as Mahalla 3, Guru Ramdas as Mahalla 4 and Guru Arjan Dev as Mahalla 5, and, finally, of Guru Tegh Bahadur as Mahalla 9. The bani of the saints follows in the same raga.

The saints whose bani has been included in the Guru Granth Sahib are Kabir, Sheikh Farid, Trilochan, Bhagat Beni, Ravidass, Namdev, Dhanna, Surdas, Jaidev, Bhikhan, Sain, Peepa, Ramanand, Parmanand, Sadhna, Satta and Balwand. Besides, there is one salok about Bhai Mardana who played the rabab for Guru Nanak. Similarly, the Swaiyyas of Bhatts have been included in the Guru Granth Sahib. Baba Farid and Baba Bheekhan were Muslims. Ramanand, Parmanand and Jaidev were Brahmins, Kabir was a weaver, Ravidass a cobbler, Sain a barber, Namdev a washerman and Sadhna a butcher.

Arrangement of Ragas in the Guru Granth Sahib
The 31 ragas included in the Guru Granth Sahib are:
1.   Siri Rag, from page 14 to 93
2.   Rag Majh, from page 94 to 150
3.   Rag Gauri, from page 151 to 346

Types of Compositions in the Guru Granth Sahib

Two kinds of compositions have been used in the Guru Granth Sahib. First, those which were then called the literary type and, second, the types which were recited in the folklore forms.

Literary Type

(a) Pada – One pada, two pada, three, four, five pada.

(b) Ashtpadi – Verses ranging from 8 lines to 21 lines.

(c) Salok – Verses of two to sixteen lines.

(d) Pauri – Pauris have various types of formations.

Folklore Type

(e) Chhant, Sohila, Ghoris, Alahunia, Anjalian, Sadd, Mundawani, Pehre, Din-raini, Vaar Sat, Thitti, Rutt, Barahmaha, Vaar etc.

There are a few compositions in the Guru Granth Sahib which do not come under the two forms recorded above and they are known by their specific names, e.g. Japuji, Anand, Sukhmani, Siddh Goshti, Dakhni Omkar etc.

Editorial Techniques of the Guru Granth Sahib

The entire bani of the Guru Granth Sahib has been recorded under the following techniques:

1. The arrangement of the raga (Chapter)
2. The serial number of the Mahalla (Guru)
3. The arrangement of the House (Ghar)
4. The arrangement of the purport (Rahao)

The chapters in the Guru Granth Sahib are made under the title of the raga. Each chapter begins with either the full Mool Mantra or a short form of it in bold letters. Then the raga is named, followed by the serial number of the Mahalla which denotes the Guru who composed it. Invariably, every chapter begins with Mahalla 1 because Guru Nanak's bani comes first.

Then the ghar is mentioned. In the Guru Granth Sahib, ghar may mean either sur or taal. Sur is the note and taal is the rhythm. There are 1 to 17 ghars, which denote the *sur and taal* of the particular composition.

Rahao literally means to pause and think. In the Guru Granth Sahib, rahao comes after the topic sentence of the composition. It reflects the significance or the intention of the composition. It contains the gist of the entire composition. In some compositions, there may be more than one rahao, which means that the central idea has changed and a new idea has been introduced.

Grammar of the Guru Granth Sahib

The intricate grammar of the Guru Granth Sahib is a full-fledged subject that needs to be studied in detail to understand the Gurbani properly. The secret of understanding the Gurbani lies in knowing the placement of the vowels. The vowels in the Gurmukhi script are as follows:

Mukta (the short vowel (a): Its use denotes the singular; the feminine nouns; and the possessive and vocative case.

Kanna (the elongated vowel (a): Its use denotes the plural.

Sihari (the short vowel (i): Its use denotes prepositions, adverbs, compound verbs, participle, conjunctive participle, imperative mood, subordinate clause, first person plural, second person plural, third person plural, pronouns, and much more.

Bihari (the elongated vowel (i): Its use denotes present perfect tense.

Aunkar (the short vowel (u): It denotes masculine singular, abstract nouns, past tense, and third person singular.

Dulainkar (the elongated vowel (u): Its use corresponds to another noun e.g. 'Vastu andar vast samavey.'

Laan (the short vowel (e): As used in the Punjabi language.

Dulaayian (the elongated vowel (e): As used in the Punjabi language.

Kanaura (the vowel (au): As used in the Punjabi language.

Nine Tunes

The following nine tunes have been prescribed along with the bani in particular ragas:

1. Vaar Majh ki Salok Mahalla 1 – *Malik Murid Chandrharha Sohia ki dhuni*
2. Gauri ki Vaar Mahalla 5 – *Rai Kamaal di Maujadi ki dhuni*
3. Vaar Asa Mahalla 1 – *Tundey Asrajey ki dhuni*
4. Gujri ki Vaar Mahalla 4 – *Sikandar Birham ki dhuni*
5. Vadhans ki Vaar Mahalla 4 – *Lala Behlima ki dhuni*
6. Ramkali ki Vaar Mahalla 3 – *Jodhey Veerai Purbani ki dhuni*
7. Sarang ki Vaar Mahalla 4 – *Rai Mahamey Hasney ki dhuni*
8. Vaar Malar Mahalla 1 – *Rane Kailas tatha Mal Deo ki dhuni*
9. Kanarhey ki Vaar Mahalla 4 – *Musey ki Vaar ki dhuni.*

These were popular tunes in which the specific epics were sung, like the specific tune in which Heer-Ranjha is sung.

For instance, let us take the tune in which Asa-di-Var is sung. The tune is called Tundey Asrajey ki dhuni. This is the story of a maimed king. His name was King Sarang. He had a beautiful son whose name was Raja Assa. He lost his mother as a babe and his father married again.

The stepmother was a cruel woman. She accused him of a crime he hadn't committed and ordered that his limbs be cut off. But the executioners were more kind. They chopped off only one hand and left him outside the precincts of the kingdom.

He wandered for many days till he reached another kingdom where he took shelter in the home of a washerman.

Many seasons went by. The king passed away without leaving an heir. The courtiers didn't know whom to make the king. Then they had a secret conference and decided on a scheme. They said, "Whoever would be the first man to enter the gate of the kingdom would become the future king."

As luck would have it, the washerman's donkey had gone missing the day before. And Assa, the servant of the washerman, came looking for it. He happened to be standing right in front of the gate when the gatekeeper opened it. He took Assa to the ministers who declared him the king without asking him who he was and where he came from.

Meanwhile, King Sarang was defeated and killed by his own half brother. The new king was very ambitious. He wanted to enhance his kingdom. So, he attacked Assa Raja's kingdom. A fierce battle followed in which Assa Raja emerged victorious.

The bards and singers of the royal court celebrated the victory. They sang in praise of the new king. The song of the king was on everyone's lips. That is why perhaps the Guru chose this tune.

Over the centuries, the ragis have sung the Asa-di-Var, the Song of Hope, in the strain prescribed by the Guru. The song is divided into twenty parts. Each canto begins with a couplet composed by Guru Nanak. It is followed by another couplet composed by Guru Angad. Then there is a verse of Guru Nanak. It concludes with a pauri of four and a half lines. Asa-di-Var is sung at dawn, in the early hours of the day.

Sheer Poetry

T he whole of the Guru Granth Sahib is composed in poetry par excellence. Poetry is a form of art in which language is used for its aesthetic and evocative qualities in addition to its meaning. Poetry uses particular forms and conventions to expand the literal meaning in the words. Devices such as similes, metaphors, symbolism, rhythm and poetic diction often leave a poem open to multiple interpretations as there are layers upon layers of meanings.

The poetry of the Guru Granth Sahib is rich in all these elements. That is why you find meanings upon meanings in the same words as you progress on the path of understanding the Gurbani.

The Guru Granth Sahib states profound truths in simple words. Take for instance, 'Man jeetey jag jeet.' Very simple indeed. But when you begin to practise it, you realise that it is perhaps the toughest thing to do. No wonder, the Gurbani brings in the same subject again and again in subsequent verses to help and guide the seeker on the path. At various instances, methods are given to keep the fleeting mind under check; like 'Man ki matt tyago har jan.' And how to do it? 'Gur satgur ki matt laini' that is, with the instruction of the Guru. And, when the mind is cleansed of all impurities, 'Man tu jot sarup hai, apna mool pachhan.' It is the ultimate stage of realisation when the mind transforms into consciousness and finds its true nature, that it is the spark of the divine light.

The economy of words in Gurbani poetry is amazing! In a couple of words, the entire concept is conveyed, which may take volumes to explain and lifetimes to practise. *'Dukh daru sukh rog bhaya,'* or *'Tu karta karna main nahi.'* If you go deep into these apparently simple words, you will realise their depth. You can go on and on, delving deeper and deeper and experience the magic of these deceptively simple phrases.

The Gurbani abounds with symbolism and imagery. Such vivid pictures are drawn in very simple words that you are left wondering at their sheer beauty. Here is an example:

'Paati toreh malini paati paati jeo.' (1328)

Picture this: "The gardener's wife goes to the garden and plucks some petals to offer at the feet of her deity, an idol that is not alive. The woman is deluding herself. She does not know that God is alive in every blade of grass. Little does she realise that she is plucking live flowers to offer at the feet of the statue made of stone! If this idol was alive, it would have objected to the sculptor when he put his foot on it to chisel it to shape it. On the other hand, the woman has offended the divine trinity since the leaf is the creator Brahma, the stem is the sustainer Vishnu and the flower is the destroyer Shankar. Who does she think she is serving?"

Similes and metaphors appear in almost every word of the Gurbani. Take this example:

'Tu dariyaao dana bina main machhali kaise ant laha.' (25)

"You are the ocean vast and deep; I am but a poor fish. How can I know you? Wherever I look, I see only you. All I know is that outside of you, I die instantly. I don't know anything about the fishing net nor about the fisherman. I only know that when I am in trouble, I remember thee. You are all around me, yet I think you are far away. Whatever I do is because of you. You are watching over me but I keep denying it. I eat whatever you provide for me; I have no one else to turn to. My only prayer is that my life is in your hands. You are near and you are far, and you are inside and outside. You see and hear everything as the world goes about doing its business. Whatever is Thy Will is happening all around."

Look at it from another angle, and the Gurbani is love poetry of the deeply passionate kind. Try and grasp this:

Antar Pyas Uthi Prabh Keri (835-36)

Guru Ramdas, the fourth Guru, speaks like a woman pining for her Beloved: "When I hear the words of my beloved, they pierce my heart like an arrow and the thirst for my beloved arises in my heart. No one can understand the pain I feel. Only I know what is happening to me inside. My beloved has stolen my heart, and I move around like a mad woman — madly in love; I have no sense of what I do and where I go.

"I go looking for my beloved here, there and everywhere because I cannot live without him. I am ready to pay any price to get just a glimpse of him. I would cut my body limb by limb if only I could set my eyes on him. I would chop off my head and place it at the feet of anyone who would take me to meet my beloved. Come, my friends, let us go and perform all the rituals and tricks that might help us win him over.

"I wear the rosary of his Naam around my neck and that is the most precious jewel for me. I had decorated the bridal bed with my devotion so that he wouldn't be able to resist the temptation. But my lord comes and says, 'Do something else; all your ornaments and adornments are hollow and meaningless.' I did all the dressing up and make up to please him but he spat at my face.

"I am your slave; you are my lord and master; what can I say; I am at your mercy. I only pray that you may take pity on me some day so that I may dissolve completely and surrender at your feet."

You can see the stages of love—love that begins with the physical love and moves on to prayer and devotion, ultimately reaching the peak in egolessness and complete surrender.

The zenith of Gurbani poetry is sublime poetry of the superlative degree.

Kot brahmand ko thakur swami (612)

"Master of innumerable worlds, you are the creator of all beings. You take care of them every moment of the day, day after day. But I am just a foolish being who is incapable of understanding even a fraction of it. I know not how to pray; I merely repeat your name. You are the compassionate merciful creator that permeates the entire cosmos. You are watching and listening to everything, but the foolish me thinks you are far away. You are endless, boundless and infinite, but I can grasp only a little bit. How do I know what you are? I pray to my Guru to show me the way, to instruct me and guide me to you. I know that criminals and sinners have been forgiven and blessed by you; I am just a stupid fool. If I get just a glimpse of you I will be free from the cycle of birth and death."

Above all, the Gurbani is meditative poetry. It creates the atmosphere in which you can go through all the stages of meditation, starting with listening, understanding, thinking, introspecting, contemplating and finally attaining that space where meditation is possible.

The Gurbani is thought-provoking. It gives you a jolt and wakes you up from your deep slumber. And, the moment you feel you have understood something, it shows another layer of itself. You struggle to get past that with much effort, and by the time you feel now you have achieved your goal, you come across the next hurdle. Very much like the elves that set out to find the end of the world. They saw the horizon and felt that they could see the end and would be able to reach it. But when they approached the scene, there was the horizon, as distant as it was when they had started their journey.

It is best illustrated by an example.

Humility is a virtue that is propagated emphatically in the Gurbani. Guru Nanak says,

Mithat neeveen Nanaka gun changiayeean tatt.

The essence of all virtues is humility.
And, again:

Neechan andar neech jat, neechi hun ati neech.
Nanak tin ke sang sath, vadian seo kya rees.

In other words, consider yourself lower than the lowliest. Compare yourself to the lowliest and don't aspire to compete with the high and mighty.

But, when you begin to inculcate humility, it tells you:

Sab ko nivey ap ko par ko nivey na koi
Dhar tarazu toliye nivey so goura hoi.

Everybody is humble for a selfish motive but no one bends to accommodate others. Still, if you compare, the humble person has more substance, like the heavier part of the scale goes down.

As you try to bring in humility in yourself and begin to think that you are a humble person, you are given another jolt:

Apradhi doona nivei jeo hanta mirgahe
Sis nivaaye kya thiye ja hriday kasudhey jaye.

It means that the criminal bends double to hide his crime like the hunter on the scent of the deer. But, merely bowing the head is meaningless if there is evil in the heart.

Thus, the Gurbani leads you on and on, step by step. You can never become complacent on the project of self-improvement because there is always scope for improvement.

In the end, it has to be admitted that poetry defies translation. And spiritual poetry of the calibre of the Gurbani is impossible to translate. This is just an attempt to give a taste of it so that the thirst arises in you and you are impelled to listen to the Gurbani in its pure and original form. And, when you listen to the musical rendition of the Gurbani, there is all the possibility that the arrow will pierce your heart and soon you will get imbued in the hue of the Gurbani.

The musical rendition of the Gurbani is called kirtan. Kirtan is the singing of the shabads of the Gurus in the prescribed ragas. All the verses in the Guru Granth Sahib can be set to music and sung. Professional singers called Raagis sing the Gurbani in the traditional way, accompanied by the harmonium (wind musical instrument) and tabla (percussion instrument).

Kirtan is a great aid to meditation. It stills the mind and raises the level of consciousness. Kirtan is not worship or prayer but helps in creating the rhythm of natural breath which enhances awareness. Whatever you do with awareness is meditation. And the Gurbani takes you into that state of awareness effortlessly. Each word of the Gurbani is rich with meaning, and when it is sung, it helps the listener go into a meditative state.

Practical Spirituality

The Guru Granth Sahib provides a blueprint of the kind of life that one should lead. It gives practical advice on how you should model your life so that you may be able to fulfill the purpose of your life and return to the source as soon as possible and as effortlessly as possible. Since the journey is from the simple to the complex, the Gurbani moves from the physical to the mental and emotional aspects of life, to finally attain the spiritual aspect.

Here is an attempt to sum up the essence of the Guru Granth Sahib:

Food and Drink

Eating is essential to maintain a healthy body. But simple eating is enough for that purpose. Too much thought and emphasis on eating is lopsided and leaves less time to do more important things in life. Plus, foods that excite the nerves are harmful as they make you lose your awareness. All intoxicants make you go astray because they are impediments in the way of gaining consciousness. Neither fasting nor feasting is recommended.

Dress

Again, simple is beautiful. Gaudy and glamorous dress has the same effect as intoxicating food. Wear the kind of dress that is comfortable and keeps the mind at peace. Dress is a social necessity. It should be treated as such. Too much emphasis on dressing up will lead you astray.

House

You need a place to call your home and that which provides the basic safety and security. But the desire to own mansions and palaces is detrimental to your growth. You are like a guest who will stay for a while and then move on. In this scheme of things, if you accumulate more, you will lose your way, you will start clinging to your belongings. That will hamper your movement and your growth. So, those who have understood this do not spend their lives hankering for bigger houses and bigger possessions. A humble hut where God is remembered is far better than a palace where He is forgotten.

The Body

The human body is a great gift; it is your opportunity to meet the Creator. You need to handle it with care. You must keep it clean from the outside by washing and bathing; and you must keep it clean from the inside by eating proper food, eating it in the right manner and doing physical exercise to digest what you have eaten.

The body is the temple of the living God. It should be treated with reverence. You should neither starve it nor overindulge it. It is the best instrument that has come to you; you must make sure that the strings of this instrument are tuned well so that good music can be produced.

Use your brain to deal with the world, but reserve your heart for the Creator. The Gurbani tells you again and again that the God you are seeking everywhere in the forests and the mountains, the temples and the gurudwaras is residing within you, in your heart. There is nowhere to go but in, in search of Him.

The Mind

The mind is the biggest illusion. It does not exist. It is the creation of your ego. It is deceptive. You need to be on your guard against it all the time otherwise it becomes your master and makes you its slave. Be aware of its crafty designs every moment.

The mind becomes very powerful because you allow it to become so. Your ego feels safe in the shadow of the mind. The mind is your alter ego; it has become stronger than you; and you feel helpless in its clutches. Without the Guru, you will find it very difficult to keep the mind in check.

The Ego

The ego is essential to know your identity, but it grows too big too soon. Then it stands like a rock in the way of your progress towards your goal. The ego is like dust in your eyes; it may not even be visible but it blinds you completely. Egoism or haumey is considered as your strongest foe with which you have to fight a battle on a daily basis. The slightest complacency on your part and it will start overcoming you. You are the rider on the horse, make sure the whip remains in your hand so that you can keep the ego under control.

Breath

Breath is life. Breath is your link between you and your Creator. Breath is the spark of divinity in you. As long as there is breath in your body, you live, you glow with its light, and you can do a myriad things. The moment breath goes out of your body, you are dead and worthless. You cannot move even your little finger, leave alone the mighty things you were capable of doing with the breath that coursed through your body.

Learn to use the breath to establish the link with your Creator. The Gurbani prescribes remembrance with every breath as the only means to attain union with the Maker. Simran or remembrance is the goal and to achieve this goal, you may use any number of methods that appeal to you and help you remember all the time. If you can use every breath to remember, you have arrived.

The Guru Granth Sahib does not prescribe any austerities, rituals or pilgrimages and prayers. It advises you to live a normal life, fulfilling the needs of the body in moderation as and when they occur, and focus only on remembrance of the Creator. In fact, it strikes at the root of superstitions and beliefs that are followed blindly.

Virtues and Vices

First of all, virtues and vices are given the importance due to them. You don't become a good person because you have certain virtues and you don't become an evil person because you have certain vices. The truth is that everybody has a combination of some virtues and some vices. The difference is only in degree and not in kind. Someone might have more virtues than vices or vice versa, but no one is free from them. Even a hardened criminal will have some virtues in him and even a saintly person will have some vices.

Virtues need to be cultivated because they help you to create a peaceful atmosphere around you so that you can pursue your goal of remembrance. On the other hand, vices create a vicious cycle and you remain trapped in it, which means you have no time for remembrance.

There are five vices that are the most difficult to deal with. They are *kam, krodh, lobh, moh, ahankar*—lust, anger, greed, attachment and pride. You are born with the gift of the spark of divinity in you. This is the precious gift that you are expected to guard vigilantly. But, these five vices are like thieves that steal your most precious treasure. You have to fight with them and get on top of them at every step in your life.

Virtues help you in creating a congenial atmosphere around you. They help you keep the ego under check. The greatest virtue is humility, which means the exact opposite of pride. A humble person will keep his ego under control. Similarly, compassion helps you to remove the suffering of others and gives you peace of mind in return. Then, instead of harming others, the Gurbani teaches you to sacrifice your own interests for others. We live in a society where the joys and sorrows of others affect us also; so if you can spread happiness all around you, you will be happy.

The Gurbani also cautions you against the pitfalls of so-called virtues. The pundits and priests who consider themselves holier-than-thou, develop an ego that becomes their greatest stumbling block. On the contrary, a simple person who has no such pretensions may be far ahead in his spiritual journey.

The entire cosmos is inter-related. What you do can have an adverse effect on somebody else, so no one is free from sin. We are all sinners in one way or another. So, accept the fact that we are sinners and pray for forgiveness. The Creator is extremely merciful and forgives us for our sins. Left to ourselves, we would never be able to clear our account.

Joys and Sorrows

Joys and sorrows are two sides of the same coin. Every person will experience joys and sorrows from time to time. But, the joy that takes you away from your purpose of life actually is the greatest sorrow. On the other hand, the sorrows that bring you back to remembrance become your greatest joy.

The Gurbani tells you to treat joys and sorrows alike. They are temporary conditions that will soon change. Like clouds in the sky, they appear for some time and then you can see the blue sky. Remember that you are the vast blue sky, and joys and sorrows come and go; you should not let them disturb your equilibrium.

Health and Disease

There are three kinds of disorders—physical sickness, when the body is sick; mental sickness, when the mind is sick; and, spiritual sickness, when the soul is sick. All these diseases imply that the natural balance has been disturbed and needs to be corrected. Disease makes you uncomfortable and, therefore, makes you lose your awareness. Physical disease is the easiest to cure because it can be detected and diagnosed easily, whereas mental disorders are more subtle and require long sessions of psychiatric treatments. Spiritual sickness is what the whole humanity is suffering from and still it is not recognised as a sickness. The Gurbani says for all such sicknesses, the only remedy is simran, remembrance. *Sarab rog ka aukhad naam.*

The very fact that you are here means that the soul has been separated from its source. It will remain in agony till it becomes one with it and returns home to the source. The journey of health is in the reverse order — if the soul is healthy, your mind and body will reflect that wellness in all its glory. No wonder, you see great sages look radiant. Every fibre in their body glows with divine light, which is present in every being but has got covered with dust to such an extent that it is not visible at all.

Pure and Impure

You do not become pure by bathing in holy rivers nor do you become pure by performing rituals. Those who think they can purify the kitchen and cook pure food with Gangajal must know that there are impurities in every food item. The Gurbani strongly condemns distinctions made on the basis of pure and polluted. If you think your food gets polluted because a person of low caste has touched it, then you must know that the water you drink has been tasted by millions of fish; the milk you drink has been tasted by the calf; the flowers you offer at the feet of the deity have been tasted by bees and butterflies. So, don't think you are purer than others just because you have bathed in the Ganga.

Friends and Foes

All human relationships are temporary; they leave you in your hour of need, which is when you will be questioned in the divine court about your deeds. So, look for the only friend who will remain by your side in this world as well as the other world. The people who criticise you are actually your friends; they are not your enemies. Your critics help you see your faults and also keep your ego under check. They are like the washerman who washes your dirty clothes. As a result, you become a better person thanks to their criticism.

True and False

If you look at it from the superficial level, then everything is false. All that is visible is false because it is temporary, short-lived. It is made of the same stuff that dreams are made of. As long as it lasts, it appears to be real, but before you know it, it is gone. However, if you can remove the veil from the face of nature, everything is true because the Creator is true, so how can his creation be false? In other words, the form is false since it keeps changing all the time. But, that which makes the form is eternal and true. The spark of divinity that runs through all the forms is true. All you need is the ability to see beyond the form and you will see that everything in His infinite creation is true.

Work and Prayer

Work is worship. An honest day's work is the best prayer. The Gurbani instructs us to do work with our hands and feet, and keep the heart attuned to remembrance. So, prayer or worship is not in lieu of work; you can pray while you are working. As a human being, it is your duty to work for your living and fulfill your responsibilities towards yourself, your family and the society. True prayer is that which arises from the heart; it has nothing to do with methods and rituals.

Life and Death

This life is your greatest opportunity; it has been granted to you after a myriad lives in different forms. The Gurbani says you have been through eighty-four lakhs of lives in the plant and animal kingdom; you have earned the human frame with great difficulty. So, don't let it go waste; it may not happen again for a long time. So make the best use of it while it is there. Use it to walk the path that leads to the divine. The longest journey, they say, is from here to here. In other words, go inwards and discover who you are.

Living in the company of mortals, you have started believing that you are going to die one day. You have lost sight of the immortal in you. Death is not the end. It is the end of the life that began with birth, whereas you have been coming and going many times before this, and will continue to do so after passing away again. Life and death are like day and night; they keep happening at regular intervals. So, don't grieve over death; make use of the rare opportunity that has been granted to you. Life is what you make of it; and your death reflects what your life has been. Live life consciously and you will die consciously too. A conscious death will take you closer to your goal. You will return home.

Heaven and Hell

The Guru Granth Sahib does not support the belief in hell and heaven. You create your own heaven and hell on this earth only. If you have a positive approach, you will look at the good even in a bad situation, whereas a negative person finds difficulties in opportunities also. And, what you do in thought, speech and action affects the world around you; you will reap what you sow. You can't plant a poisonous tree and expect nectar to grow on it, can you? You get what you deserve. So, if something bad comes your way, don't curse others for it. Instead, try to think and find out what wrong you have done for which you are being punished.

Plus, heaven is not a place; it is a state of mind. Everyone longs for peace and bliss. So, they conjure pictures of a place where all their desires will be fulfilled and they call it heaven. The Gurbani says that paradise is here and now. Listen to the Guru's word, let it sink deep into you and you will feel blessed.

Vision of the Ultimate

*T*he enlightened masters, the Gurus and saints whose spontaneous outbursts of ecstasy comprise the Guru Granth Sahib, were seers, visionaries. Seers differ from the common man because they see things as they are, whereas the common man sees them through the mind which is blurred with the dust of the prejudices, biases and conditioning of a myriad lives. The seers look beyond the mind, whereas the others see only through the mind. The seers stand out in the open looking at the whole sky, whereas the common men look at the sky through the window of the mind. The sky remains the same but we think it is the patch that is visible through the window. Vision refers to the ability to have an all-comprehensive view of the whole. Call it vision of the ultimate or the vision of the commonplace. It is the same. There is no difference between the two. Either everything is divine or everything is mundane. It is a choice of words. The truth is indivisible.

The Guru Granth Sahib sings of this vision in innumerable ways.

The first concept that materialises from the study of the Guru Granth Sahib is that the ultimate or the divine has no form, or, all the forms that exist are the forms of the divine. In other words, the forms of everything visible are apparent, whereas the reality lies hidden behind the forms. The world seems to be involved in a thousand things but the power that makes it alive remains invisible because it has no form. Or, as long as it functions through it, that is its form. And that holds good for the greatest and the smallest form. Divinity runs through the entire creation for the creator is none other than creativity itself. Like the dancer and dancing. The dancer is the dancing. They cannot be separated. An artist can paint a picture and remain separate from it, but the dancer and dancing are one. The dancer is a dancer only when he is dancing, and the dance cannot exist without the dancer. The creator is the creativity. In nature, nothing is static; everything is vibrantly dynamic. In nature, there are no nouns; there are only verbs. There is no creation but creativity, because it is changing every moment. Thus, all these dynamic forms are divine or the divine has no form.

Sahas tav nain nana nain hai tohe ko sahas murat nana ek tohi
Sahas pad bimal nana ek pad gandh bin sahas tav gandh iv chalat mohi.
Sab meh jot jot hai soi. Tisde chanan sabh meh chanan hoi.

(*GGS p.663*)

Thousands are your eyes but you have no eyes.
Thousands are your forms, but you have no form.
Thousands are your feet, but you have no feet.
Without fragrance, thousands are your fragrances.
Everything shines with your light.

Secondly, there is no space or time where the ultimate is not. This creation is full and overflowing with the divine. Guru Nanak says, '*Binay kari je duja hoi*'. I would appeal to you if you were another. There is no difference in the intrinsic nature of things and beings.

Sabhe ghat Ram boley Rama boley Ram bina ko boley re,
Ekal maati kunjar cheeti bhajan hai bahu nana re,
Asthawar jangam keet patangam ghat ghat Ram samana re,   (GGS p. 988)

Who is speaking through all the living beings? The ultimate!
The elephant or the ant; all are shapes moulded out of the same clay.
Trees and mammals, ants and insects; everything is full of the divine.

Thirdly, divinity is the nature of things. Everything is potentially divine. Remove the veil from anything and what do you find underneath? The divine! And the way to realise this truth is to look within. If one wants to know the ocean, there are two ways of doing so — either study the whole ocean or a single drop, since the drop contains the ocean. Similarly, whatever is in the universe is contained in oneself. *'Jo brahmande soi pinde.'* So if you have to look for the divine, look within. Bernard Shaw once said, "Beware of the man whose God is in the skies." The moment you conceive of a God in the heavens, you have created an unbridgeable gap between yourself and Him. God is not a person living in the skies. God is everywhere. In fact, the basic nature of the entire creation is divine because the creator and creativity are one. The Guru Granth Sahib echoes the Christian dictum of "Know thyself," or the Hindu mantra of "*Aham Brahmasi.*" Look within, for God is within you.

Kahe re ban khojan jayee,
Sarab niwasi sada alepa tohi sang samayee,
Puhap madh jeon baas basat hai mukur mahi jaise chhayee,
Taise hi hari basey nirantar ghat he khojoh bhai,

(GGS p. 684)

Why wander in the jungles in search of Him?
He who lives everywhere and is inseparable from all is clinging
to you.
Like the fragrance resides in the flower and the fire in the
coal.
He resides in you continuously. Look inside your heart.

Fourthly, the soundless sound (anhad naad) permeates the universe. That is the word, the shabad, which the sages can hear. That is the only sound of creation, the rest is noise. Those who succeed in silencing the noise of the continuously chattering mind, can listen to the eternal sound of Omkar. All the prayers only add to the noise. The real prayer can only be heard, not said. The authentic, the genuine prayer is resounding all around. The whole universe is overflowing with the sound.

Har jio gufa andar rakh ke waja pawan wajaaya
Wajaaya waja pawan nau dware pargat kiye daswa gupt rakhaya.

(*GGS p. 921*)

Your heart is the flute, the musical instrument; the wind plays
on it.
Nine are the holes that all can see; the tenth has been
mysteriously concealed.

Fifthly, the Guru Granth Sahib contains the ecstatic outpourings of devotees drenched in love. Lovers are full of love; they need to shower it. It is very difficult to love an abstraction; it is easier to realise it. The devotees of the Bhakti Movement of the medieval period sang of love and devotion. The Guru Granth Sahib is also full of verses of love—platonic and erotic. And the object of love is sometimes called the father or the master or the husband and lover. This is sheer expression of love. It does not diffuse the concept of the formless divinity.

Finally, just as the ultimate has many forms and is still formless, similarly, the divine has many names but is nameless. This is the profoundest mystery enclosed in the Guru Granth Sahib. Almost every verse in the 1,430-page holy scripture of the Sikhs mentions Naam in one way or another. Yet the ultimate is nameless. To further deepen the mystery, a variety of names of God have been repeated profusely. Ram occurs most often but other names such as Hari, Govind, Narayan, Allah, and Waheguru also occur again and again. The Muslims talk of hundred names of Allah and have a list of ninety-nine names; the hundredth is silence, no name, the nameless. The Hindus talk of thirty-three crores of names of God, implying that all names are His name or that He is nameless. The Guru Granth Sahib sings and chants Naam so often that by chanting it, one day, you can transcend it and attain the nameless divinity.

The Eternal Guru

The Guru Granth Sahib is the eternal Guru, and its relevance in the 21st century will be the same as it has been in the previous centuries, if not more. Indeed, the relevance of the Guru Granth Sahib is the relevance of truth. Truth can never become irrelevant nor can the Guru Granth Sahib ever become irrelevant because it states the truth. The 21st century has just begun; it is still in its infancy. No one can say with any amount of certainty what the future is going to be like. However, on the basis of past patterns, we can only make some predictions.

The Guru Granth Sahib guides the seeker on the path at every level. On the practical level, it lays down a certain routine, a discipline by which the daily activities may be regulated. For instance, it recommends waking up in the early hours of dawn, amrit vela. Once the day begins, the shadows of the prison house begin to fall. The time most suitable for prayer is the time when the day and night meet. The twilight hours of dusk and dawn.

Guru satguru ka jo sikh akhaye so bhalke uth har naam dhiyavey,
Udham kare bhalke parbhati isnaan kare amritsar navey.

(GGS page 305/6)

Thus, making the effort to wake up early is greatly emphasised in the Guru Granth Sahib.

Then you must take a dip to cleanse the body and at the same time wash the dust from the mind with prayers and chanting. The Guru Granth Sahib shows the path of a *grahasthi*, a householder. Nowhere does it recommend renunciation. As a householder, a man is given a fairly elaborate blueprint to guide his activities. He is to lead a normal life without any austerities. Sex is a natural instinct like thirst and hunger. A forced denial of these instincts only perpetuates them. Therefore, it is better to go through them so that it is easy to transcend them. For instance, when you are thirsty and you deny yourself a drink of water, you are not able to think of anything other than water. Thus, instead of renouncing water, you have become a helpless slave of it. The same is true for all the natural instincts. The best way to live is according to your nature or else you will become either a hypocrite or insane.

The body is the temple of the living God and must be taken care of. Just as one does not take impure things into the temple, all impurities should be avoided. In this respect, there is detailed description of what kind of food to eat, what clothes to wear and what kind of acquisitions to accumulate.

The four guiding principles of conducting life are summed up as

- *Kirat karna.*
- *Wand chhakna.*
- *Naam japna.*
- *Bhana manna.*

Kirat karna means working for one's living. Man must work for his living; the Sikh is advised to be a karmajogi.

Wand chhakna means sharing your food with others. The Sikhs have kept up the tradition of langar, the free kitchen where everyone sits together to share the food cooked in the common kitchen.

Ghal khaye kichh hathon de; Nanak rah pachhane se...

Naam japna means remembering the Creator with every breath. Though we must remain active, we must not get so involved in work that we lose sight of the truth.

Nama kahe Tilochana Hari ka naam sambhal;
Hath paon kar kaam sagal cheet Niranjan nal.

On the emotional level, detachment is recommended. Attachment is the root cause of pain. Life is beautiful if you can see it objectively. But once you get involved, the beauty is lost and you sway like a dry leaf in a storm. Ego, haumey, is the other name of attachment. The Gurbani reminds again and again that the only thing worth renouncing is the ego. Humility is the foremost virtue. Deep and heartfelt humility helps to take the sting out of the ego.

Bura jo dekhan main gaya bura na dekhya koi;
Jo dil khoja apna mujh sa bura na koi.'

Compassion for others and contentment for self is also recommended. If things go wrong for you, accept them as a gift from the master, but do not shut your eyes when you see someone else in misery. Therefore, do as much as is in your power to help the poor and the miserable. But, make sure that you remain vigilant against pride which may be just waiting outside to enter through the back door when you are not cautious. Pride will nullify all your efforts.

Fear is another debilitating emotion. The mantra is: neither fear anyone not create fear in others. It is only the fearful who make a false show of strength to create fear in others. He who is fearless, has no need to prove his strength. Acceptance, bhana, is the only way to get rid of fear. If you accept the sorrows with the joys, the failures with the successes, and pain with pleasure, with the same equanimity, then fear dissolves automatically.

On the spiritual level, the Guru Granth Sahib reveals many mysteries of life. It endeavours to help you treat your eyes so that you may be able to see the divine reality, rather than send you on a wild goose chase to seek the Creator somewhere in the clouds. 'Surati' or consciousness, awareness of things as they are helps to remove the dust from the eyes. And then you are no different from your search.

'Ram Kabira ek bhaye hain koi na sake pachhani.'

The 21st century, which at this point of time shows signs of being a highly materialistic age, may just take a turn for spirituality. In the natural course of things, when a certain trend reaches its saturation point, it turns back with the same force. On that assumption, it will not take too long for humanity to turn towards spiritualism and then the Guru Granth Sahib will, perhaps, be sought after more than other scriptures because it brings the latest news from the heavens.

The poetry and music of the Guru Granth Sahib is beyond compare. Meticulously compiled and arranged into 5,894 hymns, the Adi Granth is set equally meticulously to 31 ragas of the classical music tradition, which has a "powerful appeal to the heart as much as the mind."

The tradition of kirtan has been kept up not only in the gurudwaras but also in homes. Guru Arjan Dev is said to have blessed the Sikhs with this talent when he declared that every Sikh will be able to do kirtan. No wonder, kirtan forms an essential part of any ceremony in Sikh homes. With the advanced technologies, kirtan is available to all and sundry. The 21st century will revel in the music of the Guru Granth Sahib. It is difficult to remain untouched by the verses of the Guru Granth Sahib sung in classical ragas.

Approaching the Guru

It is an extraordinary miracle that the Guru is so easily available, but we must know how to approach the Guru in order to derive the maximum benefit. Here are a few hints:

A Specific Room

The first and foremost thing to do is to make a place for the Guru in your home. It is important to allocate a specific area where you want to enshrine the Guru Granth Sahib. This is the place where you will be reading, reciting, singing and, most importantly, listening to the Gurbani. Soon, you will realise that the room will acquire a special vibe, the atmosphere will be charged and it will make simran or remembrance easier and spontaneous for you.

Installation

Guru Arjan Dev ji placed the Guru Granth Sahib on a peerhee (a small bed) and spread a cover over it. That is the tradition followed till date. It is significant because it inspires reverence in the heart of the devotee. Just as you would take care of anything valuable, you will want to do all that is necessary for the home of your Guru to be the best in every respect.

It will neither add anything to the Guru's stature nor take anything from it. *Vada na hovey ghaat na jaaye.* The Guru is not dependent on your respect or lack of it. But, the love and devotion you extend towards your Guru will go a long way in creating that atmosphere in which you can gain something from the Guru.

It is like taking a well-scrubbed pot to fetch water from the well. Your pot makes no difference to the water of the well, but it certainly makes a lot of difference to what you bring from it. So, make sure that your pitcher is clean, empty, and face up. Then the Gurbani will flow into it and you will start overflowing with it.

Parkash and Waaq (Hukamnama)

The tradition to do parkash in the morning and sukhasan in the evening is also very meaningful. Parkash means to open the Guru Granth Sahib randomly and read the shabad that is on that particular page. This is the best way to begin the day. It helps you put things in perspective. It has the power to lift you to a higher level of consciousness so that the problems that seemed too big a moment ago seem to have become small if they have not totally evaporated. As you listen to the order of the day, you will be surprised many times because it seems as if it is meant only for you. As you proceed, you will find much more than you ever imagined.

Sukhasan

In the evening, after the evening prayer, you put the Guru Granth Sahib to rest. The shabad you read at the close of the day stays with you throughout the night. It revolves in your head and resounds in your heart, giving you guidance and enhancing your experience.

Akhand Path and Sahaj Path

The tradition of reading the entire Guru Granth Sahib non-stop is called Akhand Path. Reading is done on rotation so that there is no interruption in the continuous flow of the Gurbani. The reading is completed in forty-eight hours. This has its own charm as it is like a flowing river from which you can take a drink any time you like.

Sahaj Path is done leisurely during the day over a period of time. It gives you more time to listen and absorb the Gurbani. Akhand Path and Sahaj Path are usually done by trained pathis (readers of the Guru Granth Sahib) to make sure that they pronounce the Gurbani correctly.

Pronunciation

The Guru Granth Sahib is written entirely as poetry. The grammar of the Guru Granth Sahib is extremely intricate. It is not an easy task to learn the correct pronunciation of the words and the right intonation. You need to listen to the Gurbani being recited and sung before you attempt to read it yourself. If you mispronounce the words or miss the delicate nuances of intonation, you may not understand it at all, or worse still, you may derive the wrong meaning from it. Fortunately, audio and video tapes and CDs are available that give you a taste of the Gurbani.

Surrender

The tradition to bow your head before the Guru is very significant. It implies that you surrender your head at the feet of your Guru, and are ready to accept his order unconditionally. Bowing your head before the Guru is symbolic of complete surrender. Unfortunately, it has become a hollow ritual for most people who never go beyond bowing their head to read and listen to what the Guru is saying.

Lead Kindly Light

Bani guru guru hai bani vich bani amrit sarey
Gurbani kahey sewak jan maney partakh guru nistarey

The Guru Granth Sahib is the living Guru. It can guide you at every step and lead you effortlessly to your goal, if you know how to follow your Guru. And, this is a big 'if'. The Guru Granth Sahib abounds in treasures; you have to know how to pick them up and make use of them. Therefore, the way you approach your Guru is of utmost importance, otherwise you will remain bereft of all that it offers.

The best part is that the Gurbani itself tells you again and again how to approach it and follow it, and what you stand to gain from it. Here we will analyse one shabad and see how it goes:

Ratna rattan padarth bauh sagar bharya Ram
Bani gurbani lagey tin hath charya Ram. (442)

The Gurbani is like the ocean that houses innumerable precious gems. Those who can dive deep into the ocean, will find these treasures. Those who go really deep, will be able to discover all the secrets. The Gurbani will fill your heart with devotion and then you will go deep within your self and discover the ultimate secret, which is that the Guru and God are one; there is no difference between the two.

In order to let the Guru Granth Sahib guide you and lead you, you need to get familiar with the path you will be walking with the Guru. The Gurbani is as vast and as deep as the ocean. What we get from it depends on the pitcher we take to fill in it. The basic requirements to get something from this vast ocean of practical wisdom and mystic spirituality are:

The first requirement is that our pitcher (mind) should not be upside down. You have to keep it face up in order to get something in it. If you keep your pitcher upside down, then all the rain that falls on it will not be able to fill it up no matter what precious metal your pitcher is made of. You have to make sure that it faces in the right direction. The example given in the Gurbani is that of the bird chatrik that opens its beak and waits for the rain drop to fall in it because its thirst for water is so intense. That is the kind of intensity required from a gurmukh, which literally means that he faces the Guru and obeys his command, not allowing his ego to come in the way. On the other hand, a manmukh is the person who turns his back towards the sun and says that there is no such thing as light.

Secondly, your pitcher should be clean, otherwise whatever you get in it will be soiled with what was already there in the pitcher. The mind is by nature too full of the trivial. It keeps accumulating dust. It needs to be cleaned on a daily basis, just as you scrub and clean the pots and pans in the kitchen. We scrub and clean our body also every day but we forget that the mind needs a similar exercise more urgently. It has to be emptied of the myriad messages that the senses bring to it every moment. Though it is almost impossible to empty the mind completely, you can at least take a heart full of devotion when you go to the Guru and you will receive in plenty.

Listening

Thirdly, you need to be able to listen, which is the first step. But you cannot listen till you are silent, otherwise you hear your own voice louder than any other sound. Listening is an art that can be learnt. It is very different from hearing. You hear everything and still remain the same, whereas you can be totally transformed if you can listen to even one word. Such listening is possible only when you set aside your entire way of thinking, which involves selective hearing of things that are consistent with your thoughts. All else just falls on deaf ears. Your vessel is greasy; words fall on it, but they slide off, leaving you untouched.

So you are not truly listening but only lending your ears to what agrees with you and strengthens your opinion. The rest you ignore and forget. Even if you do happen to hear something contrary to your understanding, you tear it to bits with your reasoning, because you are convinced of one thing: whatever matches with your thoughts is correct; what doesn't is incorrect, false.

Another way to escape listening is to fall asleep when something significant is being said. This is a trick the mind uses to save itself; it is a very deep process by which, when something is about to touch you, you fall asleep. Sleep is like the soldier's armour; it protects you against all you don't want to know. So you look as if you are listening but you are not awake; and without being awake, how can you hear?

While talking, you are awake; while listening, you are not. As soon as another person talks to you, you are no longer alert but lost in an internal dialogue of your own. You are thinking of what to say to him.

He alone is capable of listening who has broken this inner dialogue. If the internal dialogue stops even for a moment, you find the whole expanse of space opening within you; all that was as yet unknown begins to be known. And it happens so suddenly.

When you learn the art of listening, you attain all; death does not touch you, you are the master of all occult powers and the whole world exists because of listening.

How is this internal dialogue to be broken? How can the clouds be made to disappear so that the clear skies can be seen?

By becoming silent.

When you came into this world, you were silent. Prepare to leave it in silence, too. Talking is relevant in the mundane world; it is useful for relating to another person. But it is madness to talk to yourself. Talking is a bridge that connects you to others; silence is a bridge that connects you with yourself.

Have you ever wondered why does this internal dialogue go on?

It is out of habit. From day one, you have been taught to speak. Talking is a social art and is necessary for living in society. You are so habituated to talking that you talk even in sleep. You keep on talking and rehearsing. Before talking to someone, you rehearse the dialogue internally; and after the conversation, you repeat it over and over again. Externally, you may be gaining something, but within you are certainly losing contact with yourself. And the more adept you become at this game, the harder it is for you to retreat into silence.

When you walk, you use your legs; while sitting, there is no need to move your legs. When you communicate with others, you need to talk, but there is no need to talk when you are alone.

Listening is a passive state. You have to do nothing to listen. In order to see, you have to open your eyes but the ears are already open. You have nothing to do in order to hear. Hence, there is some sense of doing in seeing, but hearing does not involve doing at all. Someone speaks. You listen, sitting empty, motionless, passive; you are in non-action.

Listening is the other side of silence. There is a solitude in moments of listening in which a voice resounds and passes away. There is no one within. If a thought comes, you come along with it; when thoughts are not, you are not. That is the egoless state of samadhi.

On the tracks to the divine, the first and foremost step is of listening. Listening is given utmost importance. Guru Nanak has devoted four pauris to listening in Japuji. Listening can do wonders. However, there are a few requisites to be able to listen properly. Unless you are completely silent inside, you will miss listening and that is what happens all the time. You are so full of noise that you hardly manage to listen to a fraction of what you hear. The mind is always chattering incessantly. If you are honest to yourself, you will know that the mind is always chattering. There are many voices competing with one another to gain your attention. It is a common experience that when you sit down to pray, meditate or listen to the Gurbani, your mind is full of noise. The truth is that the mind is always full of noise; you realise it only when you stop for a moment to pray or meditate.

Thus, silence is a necessary condition to be able to listen. Secondly, you need to give up your preconceived notions before you can listen to your Guru. You have images and associations about everything that become a wall between you and what you hear. You need to cleanse your mind and get rid of all such beliefs, opinions and notions to be able to listen properly.

The next four pauris in Japuji are devoted to acceptance — total and unconditional.

Acceptance

Acceptance is considered the supreme virtue in the Gurbani. Acceptance means having faith in the scheme of things. It means knowing that whatever is happening is right and whatever is right is happening.

Listening to the Guru and accepting every word of it is the only way to let your Guru lead you. *Salam jawab dovey karey muddon bhukha jaaye.* You cannot bow before your Guru and then question him. If you do so, you return as empty as you came to him. If you want your Guru to guide you, you will have to accept him wholeheartedly.

Eho bani jo jio jaaney tis antar vasey hari nama.
Kahat sunat sabhey sukh pavey, maanat pavey nidhana.

By reading and listening to the Gurbani, you can find all the joys of this world but by accepting His Word, you will find the true treasure.

Surrender

The Gurbani is pure poetry and music. Let it sink into your heart and soul. The more you listen to it, the more you will want to go deep into it. Soon you will realise its magic, when you will feel the Gurbani flowing from your heart like music from a flute. You will find deeper and deeper meanings in the same words. So, make your heart like a hollow bamboo so that the Creator plays on it and creates celestial music. Surrender yourself completely to your Guru and he will lead you all the way. The Guru is benevolent and always willing to help if only we can leave our ego outside when we come in the presence of the Guru just like we take off our shoes outside before we enter a gurudwara.

Japuji

Ek Omkar

Satnam

Karta Purukh

Nirbhau

Nirwair

Akal Murat

Ajooni

Saibham

Gurprasad.

Omkar is the all-pervading sound
The only one that pervades all around
It is the only truth that exists
For it is, has been and ever will be.

The creator and the creation are one
Like the seed and the tree are one
The only difference being that
One is contained in the other.

Creativity can never be fearful or biased
Creativity is beyond birth or death
Creativity is without a beginning or an end
Continuity is the criterion of creativity.

Creativity is totally independent
Creativity exists by itself
The potential and the unseen
Is also the visible and the manifest.

The ability to see the potential
Comes with the grace of the Guru
When the Guru showers his blessings
One sees the divine in everything.

Japu

Aad sach jugaad sach.
Hai bhi sach Nanak hosi bhi sach.

Sochey soch na hovayee je sochi lakh var.
Chupey chup na hovayee je laye raha liotar.

Bhukhia bhukh na uttari jy banna purian bhar.
Sahas siyanapa lakh hoye ta ik na chale nal.

Kiv sachiara hoyeeyeh kiv kurheh tutey pal.

Hukam rajayee chalna Nanak likhia nal. // 1 //

Japu

You are and have been since ages
You are as true as you have always been

I cannot grasp you through my mind
Even if I think a hundred thoughts
I cannot silence the chattering of the mind
Even if I vow never to speak again.

Just as any number of thoughts of food
Cannot allay the pangs of hunger
Similarly, all wisdom is of no use
When it comes to knowing you.

Then what can bring me closer to truth?
What is it that can purify me inside out?
What will break the wall of falsehood?
It is the acceptance of the Divine Will!

Hukmi hovan akar hukam na kahia jayee.

Hukami hovan jee hukam miley vadiyayee.

Hukami uttam neech hukam likh dukh sukh payeeyeh.

Ikna hukmi bakhsis ik hukmi sada bhavayeeyeh.

Hukameh andar sabh ko bahar hukam na koi.

Nanak hukameh je bujhey ta haumey kahe na koi. // 2 //

The divine will is the order
In which forms are created
Unquestioned, it prevails above all
And creation continues unhindered.

Man is the latest addition
He has created the dual throng
Distinguishing between high and low
Between sins and virtues, and so on.

The Divine Will blesses some
While others come and go.
But there is none outside of it
He who realises the Divine Will with the Guru's grace
His ego disappears without a trace.

Gavey ko tan hovey kise tan.
Gavey ko daat janey nisan.

Gavey ko gunn vaddiayayeean char.
Gavey ko vidya vikham vichar.

Gavey ko saaj kare tan kheh.
Gavey ko jee lai phir deh.

Gavey ko jaapey disey door.
Gavey ko vekhey hadra hadoor.

Kathna kathi na aavey tot.
Kath kath kathi koti kot kot.

Deinda de lainde thak payey.
Juga juguntar khahi khahey.

Hukmi hukam chalaey rah.
Nanak vigsey veparvah. // 3 //

He who is blessed sings
He who recognises sings
Overflowing with gratitude
He sings and sings in appreciation.

Some marvel at the body
While others marvel at the mind
Yet others wonder about the power
That makes the mind and body move

Some see the divine close by
While others worship a god in the sky

But all of them sing
The song never ending
Like the song of nature
Sung by each and every being.

They sing of the beauty of creativity
That gives and gives untiringly
Even though the takers tire of taking
Over centuries and for generations.

Creativity is never ending
Nanak thrives on it.

Sacha Sahib sach naaye bhakhya bhao apar.
Aakhey mangey de de daat kare datar.
Pher ki aggey rakhiye jit disey darbar.
Muhon ki bolan boliye jit sunn dharey pyar.

Amrit vela sach nao vaddiayee vichar.
Karmi aavey kapra nadri mokh dwar.
Nanak eivey janeeye sabh aape sachiar. // 4 //

Thapia na jaye kita na hoi.
Aape aap niranjan soi.
Jin seweya tin paya maan.
Nanak gaveeye gunni nidhan.

Gaveeye suneeye mann rakhiye bhao.
Dukh parhar sukh ghar lei jaye.

Gurmukh naadan gurmukh vedan gurmukh rahya samayee.
Gur eesar gur gorakh barma gur parbati mayee.

Je hau jana akha nahi kahna kathan na jayee.
Gura ik de bujhayee.
Sabhna jian ka ik data so main visar na jayee. // 5 //

Nanak says what can I offer you?
You have given me everything.
What is mine that I can offer to you?
What can I say that will bring me closer to you?

Listen to the song of nature
In the early hours of dawn
It will purify the physical frame
Granted as a boon to man alone.

Sing in tune with nature's song
That has no shape or form
That pervades the whole universe
Sing to the all pervasive deity.

Singing, listening and contemplating
Will free you of all sorrows and miseries

The all-pervasive deity is my Guru
His word is all the scriptures put together
He is theVedas and Upanishads for me
His word is the gods and goddesses for me.

Even if I know you I cannot tell
I have not the ability to express in words.
Grant me but one wish, my Lord!
Let me never forget the creator of all.

Teerath nahva je tis bhava vin bhane ke nayee karee.
Jeti sirathi upayee vekha vin karma ke miley layee.
Matt vich ratan jawahar manik je ik gur ki sikh sunee.

Gura ik de bujhayee.
Sabhna jian ka ik data so main visar na jayee. // 6 //

Je jug chare aarja hor dasooni hoi.
Nava khanda vich janeeye naal chale sabh koi.
Changa nao rakhai ke jas keerat jag lei.
Je tis nadar na aavayee ta vaat na puchhey kei.

Keeta andar keet kar dosi dos dharey.
Nanak nirgun gunn kare gunnvantya gunn dei.
Teha koi na sujhyee je tis gunn koi karei. // 7 //

With your blessings I become pious
Without bathing in the holy waters.
With your blessings I attain
The greatest treasures of all kinds.

Grant me but one wish, my Lord!
Let me never forget the creator of all.

Even if I were to live for centuries
Even if I were known far and wide
Even if I achieved fame and success
Without your favour I am naught.

I am smaller than the tiniest ant
I am a sinner unforgivable
But you forgive the sinner that I am
Because you are the merciful lord.

Sunniye sidh pir surnath.
Sunniye dharat dhawal aakas.

Sunniye deep lo patal.
Suneeye poh na sakey kal.

Nanak bhagta sada vigas.
Suneeye dookh paap ka nas. // 8 //

Suneeye eesar barma ind.
Suneeye mukh salahan mand.

Suneeye jog jugat tan bhed.
Suneeye sasat simrat ved.

Nanak bhagta sada vigas.
Suneeye dookh paap ka nas. // 9 //

Listen to the all pervading sound
It opens all doors of knowledge
Listen to the all pervading sound
It makes all worlds visible to you.

Listen to the all pervading sound
It reveals the deepest secrets of life.
Listen to the all pervading sound
It eradicates the fear of death and beyond.

Listen to the all pervading sound
And remain in a permanent state of bliss.
Listening to it the devotees rejoice
They are free of all sorrows and sins.

Listen to the all pervading sound
And surpass all gods and goddesses
Listen to the all pervading sound
And know all the scriptures.

Listen to the all pervading sound
And know the secrets of salvation.
Listening to it the devotees rejoice
They are free of all sins and sorrows.

Suneeye sat santokh gyan.
Suneeye athsath ka isnan.

Suneeye parh parh pavey maan.
Suneeye lagey sahaj dhyan.

Nanak bhagta sada vigas.
Suneeye dookh paap ka nas. // 10 //

Suneeye sara gunna ke gah.
Suneeye sekh pir patsah.

Suneeye andhe pavey rah.
Suneeye hath hovey asgah.

Nanak bhagta sada vigas.
Suneeye dookh paap ka nas. // 11 //

Listen to the all pervading sound
And know truth and contentment
Listen to the all pervading sound
It is as good as bathing in holy rivers.

Listen to the all pervading sound
It helps you go deep in meditation.
It is better than learning and erudition.
It is better than kingdoms temporal and spiritual

Listening to it the devotees rejoice
They are free of all sins and sorrows.

Listen to the all pervading sound
The blind have found their way with it
Listen to the all pervading sound
The ignorant have found answers profound

Listening to it the devotees rejoice
They are free of all sins and sorrows.

Manney ki gat kahi na jaye.
Je ko kahe pichhe pachhtaye.
Kagad kalam na likhanhar.
Manney ka beh kare vichar.

Aisa naam niranjan hoi.
Je ko mann jane mann koi. // 12 //

Manney surat hovey mann budh.
Manney sagal bhavan ki sudh.
Manney muh chota na khaye.
Manney jamm ke sath na jaye.

Aisa naam niranjan hoi.
Je ko mann jane mann koi. // 13 //

Manney marag thak na paye.
Manney pat sio pargat jaye.
Manney mag na chale panth.
Manney dharam seti sanbandh.

Aisa naam niranjan hoi.
Je ko mann jane mann koi. // 14 //

Manney paveh mokh dwar.
Manney parvarey sadhar.
Manney tare taare gur sikh.
Manney Nanak bhavey na bhikh.

Aisa naam niranjan hoi.
Je ko mann jane mann koi. // 15 //

Acceptance of the divine will is the key
He who accepts unconditionally attains
No one can describe his state of bliss
If you try, you will only go amiss.

Such is the quality of the divine sound
Only he knows who is absorbed in it.

He who accepts lives in full consciousness
He who accepts uncovers the mysteries
He is elevated to a realm above miseries
He who accepts thy will conquers death.

Such is the quality of the divine sound
Only he knows who is absorbed in it.

He who accepts the divine will is free
He is free from rules and regulations
He is free from instructions and dictations
And from organisations and institutions
He is in touch with religion in its natural form.

Such is the quality of the divine sound
Only he knows who is absorbed in it.

He who accepts the divine will attains
He arrives home honoured and acclaimed
He is free from the cycle of birth and death
He is an inspiration for all concerned.

Such is the quality of the divine sound
Only he knows who is absorbed in it.

74

Panch parvan panch pardhan.
Panche pavey dargah maan.
Panche sohe dar rajan.
Pancha ka gur ek dhyan.

Je ko kahe kare vichar.
Karte kai karne nahi sumar.
Dhaul dharam daya ka poot.
Santokh thap rakhya jin soot.
Je ko bujhey hovye sachiar.
Dhavale upar keta bhar.
Dharti hor parey hor hor.
Tis te bhar taley kavan jor.
Jee jaat ranga ke naav.
Sabhna likhya vurhi kalaam.
Eh lekha likh jaaney koi.
Lekha likhya keta hoi.
Keta taan suaaleyo roop.
Keti daat janey kaun koot.

Keeta pasao eko kawao.
Tis te hoi lakh dareao.

Kudrat kavan kaha vichar.
Varya na java ek var.
Jo tudh bhavey sai bhali kar.
Tu sada salamat nirankar. // 16 //

He who knows is the real leader
He is respected in the divine abode
He is recognised by the royal courts
No one can sing enough of his glories.

No one has the capacity to tell
What time or place did creation begin?

There are myriad stories and theories
Suffice it to know it is all the divine will.

The intellectuals build theories
That explain less and confuse more

One question leads to another
No one knows the answers.

Everyone has tried to explain
But no one has come to any conclusion
Their efforts go in vain
Confounding the confusion.

It is the one and only sound
That is manifest in myriad ways

All I know is that nature is true
And whatever is, is your form.
Whatever is, is thy will
I am wonder struck by it!

Asankh jap asankh bhao.
Asankh puja asankh tap tao.
Asankh granth mukh ved path.
Asankh jog man rahe udas.
Asankh bhagat gunn gyan vichar.
Asankh sati asankh datar.
Asankh soor muh bhakh sar.
Asankh maun liv laye tar.

Kudrat kavan kaha vichar.
Varya na java ek var.
Jo tudh bhavey sai bhali kar.
Tu sada salamat nirankar. // 17 //

Asankh murakh andh ghor.
Asankh chor haramkhor.
Asankh amar kar jaye jor.
Asankh gal vadd hatya kamaye.
Asankh paapi paap kar jaye.
Asankh kurhiar kurhe phiraye.
Asankh malechh mal bhakh khaye.
Asankh nindak sir karey bhar.

Nanak neech kahe vichar.
Varya na java ek var.
Jo tudh bhavey sai bhali kar.
Tu sada salamat nirankar. // 18 //

Millions pray to you through austerities
Millions are your devotees deeply in love
Millions recite the scriptures day and night
Millions renounce the world in search of light
Millions sing your praises
Millions die fighting in the battlefield
Millions die on the funeral pyre
Millions sit silently in meditation.

All I know is that nature is true
And whatever is, is your form.
Whatever is, is thy will
I am wonderstruck by it!

Millions sin in ignorance
Millions steal, rob and kill
Millions cheat and deceive
Millions sin and get away
Millions go astray
Millions condemn and criticise.
Millions soil their body and mind

All I know is that nature is true
And whatever is, is your form.
Whatever is, is thy will
I am wonderstruck by it!

Asankh naav asankh thaav.
Agam agam asankh lo.
Asankh kahe sir bhar hoi.

Akhri naam akhri salah.
Akhri gyan geet gunn gah.
Akhri likhan bolan baan.
Akhra sir sanjog vakhaan.

Jin eh likhey tis sir nahe.
Jiv phurmaye tiv tiv pahe.
Jeta kita teta nao.
Vin navey nahi ko thao.

Kudrat kavan kaha vichar.
Varya na java ek var.
Jo tudh bhavey sai bhali kar.
Tu sada salamat nirankar. // 19 //

Bhariye hath paer tan deh.
Pani dhotey utras kheh.
Moot paleeti kapar hoi.
De sabun layeeye oh dhoi.
Bhariyeeye matt paapa ke sung.
Oh dhope naave ke rung.

Punni paapi aakhan nahe.
Kar kar karna likh lei jahu.
Aape beej aape hee khahu.
Nanak hukmi aavhu jaahu. // 20 //

Millions is just a word
Not even appropriate to grasp
It is folly to try to measure
That which is immeasurable.

But words are the only medium
For thinking and for singing
For writing and for speech
To describe the bond that exists
Between the divine and the mundane.

But no one knows the Writer
No one can read the Writing
Creativity spreads all around
And we are drowned in it.

All I know is that nature is true
And whatever is, is your form.
Whatever is, is thy will
I am wonderstruck by it!

When the body gets dirty
Wash it with water and it's clean
When clothes get soiled or stained
Wash them clean with soap and detergent
When the mind is full with sin
Wash it clean with love and affection.

Sins and virtues are not mere words
Our deeds are recorded meticulously
We reap whatever we sow
And that determines how we come and go.

Teerath tap daya datt dan.
Je ko paavey til ka maan.
Sunya mannya mann kita bhao.
Antargat teerath mal nao.

Sabh gunn tere main nahi koi.
Vin gunn keetey bhagat na hoi.
Suwast aath bani barmao.
Sat suhan sada mann chao.

Kavan so vela vakhat kavan kavan thiti kavan vaar.
Kavan so rutti mah kavan jit hoya akar.
Vel na paya punditi je hovey lekh puran.
Vakhat na payo kadiya je likhan lekh quran.
Thiti vaar na jogi jane rutt mah na koyee.
Ja karta sirthi ko saaje aape janey soyee.

Kiv kar aakha kiv salahi kio varni kiv jana.
Nanak akhan sabh ko akhey ik du ik sayana.
Vada sahib vadi naie kita ja ka hovey.
Nanak je ko aapo jane aggey gaya na sohey. // 21 //

Pilgrimages, charities and austerities
All are nothing in comparison
To accepting the divine will
Willingly and unconditionally.

Creativity is whole; we are only parts
Without acceptance of His Will there is no devotion.
I salute the all-pervading sound
That is the only truth beneath all visible forms.

No one can claim to know the beginning
They can only make conjectures
Neither the Vedas nor the Puranas
Have given a date or time when it began.
Neither the mullah nor the yogi
Knows anything about it.
Only the Creator knows his secret.

How can I describe you; I have no words
Even the most intelligent ones fail to say anything
Creativity is an ongoing process
That is the secret of existence.

Patala patal lakh agasa agaas.
Orak orak bhal thakey ved kahan ik vaat.
Sahas atharah kahan kateba asalu ik dhaat.
Lekha hoi ta likheeye lekhey hoi vinaas.
Nanak vada aakheeye aape janey aap. // 22 //

Salahi salah eti surat na payeeya.
Nadiya ate vah paveh samund na janeeyeh.
Samund sah sultan girha seti maal dhan.
Keeree tul na hovni je tis manhu na veesereh. // 23 //

Ant na sifti kahan na ant.
Ant na karne dein na ant.
Ant na vekhan sunnan na ant.
Ant na japey kya mann mant.
Ant na japey kita akar.
Ant na japey paravar.

Ant kaaran kete billahey.
Taakey ant na paye jahey.
Eh ant na janey koi.
Bahuta kaheeye bahuta hoi.

Vada sahib ucha thao.
Uche upar ucha nao.
Eivad ucha hovey koi.
Tis uche ko janey soi.
Jevad aap janey aap aap.
Nanak nadri karmi daat. // 24 //

There are innumerable worlds
Below the sea and above the sky
Millions living in them
Have tried to seek the truth.

Millions sing your eulogies
But they do not have a clue
Like the river cannot tell
The depth of the sea.
Not all the kings and emperors
Are as powerful as an ant
That never forgets thee.

There is no end to the donors giving generously
There is no end to the worshippers praying incessantly
There is no end to the scholars writing scriptures
There is no end to the eulogisers singing praises.

They are struggling to find the end
They have not the slightest clue
No one knows anything about it
The more they try, the more they are confused.

This is the business of love
He who loves dissolves without a trace
He becomes one with the existence.
Neither the gods nor man
Can see the difference
In him and the existence.

Bahuta karam likhia na jaye.
Vada data til na tamaye.
Kete mangeh jodh apar.
Ketia ganat nahi vichar.
Kete khap tuteh vekar.
Kete lei lei mukar pahey.
Kete murakh khahi khahey.
Ketia dookh bhookh sadd mar.
Eh bhi daat teri datar.

Bandh khalasi bhane hoi.
Hor aakh na sakey koi.
Je ko khayak aakhan paye.
Oh janey jetia muh khaye.

Aape janey aape dei.
Aakhey se bhi keyee kei.
Jisno bakhseh sifat salah.
Nanak patsahi patsah. // 25 //

Creation cannot be summed up in deeds
It is too varied to be captured in words
Many long to become brave
Others seek knowledge
Many waste their life in indulgence.
Many receive and deny
Many fools remain involved in folly
Many suffer from hunger and pain.
All this is also your creation.

He who accepts it in totality
He alone is liberated fully
Anything short of this
Is mere deception and delusion.

The Almighty Lord knows
He blesses those who surrender
They dissolve their egos
They are the real kings and emperors.

Amul gunn amul vapar.
Amul vapariye amul bhandar.
Amul aaveh amul lai jahey.
Amul bhaye amula samahey.
Amul dharam amul deeban.
Amul tul amul parvan.
Amul bakhsis amul neesan.
Amul karam amul phurman.
Amulo amul aakhya na jaye.
Aakh aakh rahe liv laye.
Aakheh ved path puran.
Aakheh parhey kare vikhyan.
Aakheh barmey aakheh ind.
Aakheh gopi te govind.
Aakheh eesar aakheh sidh.
Aakheh kete keete budh.
Aakheh danav aakheh dev.
Aakheh sur nar muni jan sev.
Kete aakheh aakhan paye.
Kete keh keh uth uth jaye.
Ete keete hor kareh.
Ta aakh na sakey kei ke.

Jevad bhavey tevad hoi.
Nanak janey sacha soi.
Je ko aakhey bol vigar.
Ta likhiye sir gavara gavar. // 26 //

Priceless are those who deal in virtues.
Priceless are they who buy virtues.
Priceless is the court and the law divine
Priceless is the scale and the measures
Priceless are those that have been forgiven
Priceless are the actions that have been accepted

These superior beings cannot be counted.
They have attained and have become silent.

The Vedas and Puranas are describing it
They read and interpret it in many ways
Brahma and Indra are singing its praises
Krishna and gopis are singing the same song

The saints and sages are singing
The siddhas, buddhas and gods are singing
The giants and monsters are also singing
The rishis, munis and goddesses are singing.

They sing all their life and pass on
But the song goes on and on.

They sing about what they see
They are the truly blessed
Others talk to make noise
They have nothing to say.

So dar keha so ghar keha jit beh sarab samaley.
Vajey naad anek asankha kete vavanharey.
Kete rag pari sio kaheeye kete gavanharey.

Gaveh tuhno paun pani baisantar gaveh raja dharam dwarey.
Gaveh chit gupt likh janey likh likh dharam vicharey.
Gaveh eesar barma devi sohan sada sawarey.
Gaveh ind indasan baithey devtiyan dar naley.
Gaveh sidh samadhi andar gavan sadh vicharey.
Gavan jati sati santokhi gaveh veer kararey.
Gavan pundit parhan rakhisar jug jug veda naley.
Gaveh mohaniyan man mohan surga machh piyaley.
Gavan ratan upaye tere athsath teerath naley.
Gaveh jodh mahabal sura gaveh khani charey.
Gaveh khand mandal varbhanda kar kar rakheh dharey.

Seyee tudhno gaveh jo tudh bhaavan ratey tere bhagat rasaley.
Hor kete gavan se main chit na aavan Nanak kya vicharey.

Soi soi sada sach sahib saacha saachi nayee.
Hai bhi hosi jaye na jaasi rachna jin rachaayee.

Rangi rangi bhaati kar kar jinsi maya jin upaayee.
Kar kar vekhey keeta apna jiv tis di vadiyayee.

Jo tis bhaveh soi karsi hukam na karna jayee.
So patsah saha patsahib Nanak rahan rajayee. // 27 //

The divine abode is where
Myriad instruments are playing
And the entire creation is singing
Myriad are the ragas and the tunes

The air, water and fire are singing
The kings and judges are singing
Chitragupt and Dharam Rai are singing
Ishwar, Brahma, and Indra are singing.
The soldiers and warriors are singing
The sages in meditation are singing
The scholars and writers are singing
The pundits and priests are singing
The beautiful fairies are singing
Countries, continents and universes are singing
The gods and goddesses are singing
The suns and stars are singing
The forests and mountains are singing
Where the birds and insects are singing

Only they can sing who have your blessings
I cannot name all the singers that are singing.
Nanak knows that only he is singing
Through all the innumerable singers.
He has created them and given them voice.
All the singers will come and go
You keep watching the scene below
Untouched by what is happening
Your creation lives as per your law.
The true king is he who abides by it.

Munda santokh saram patt jholi
dhyan ki kare bibhut.
Khintha kal kuwari kaya
jugat danda parteet.
Aayee panthi sagal jamati
 man jeetey jag jeet.

Aades tisey aades.
Aad aneel anaad anahat jug jug eko ves. // 28 //

Bhugat gyan daya bhandaran
ghat ghat vajey naad.

Aap nath nathi sabh jaki
 ridh sidh avra saad.
Sanjog viyog doi kaar chalaveh
 lekhey aaveh bhaag.

Aades tisey aades.
Aad aneel anad anahat jug jug eko ves. // 29 //

Eka mayee jugat viaayee tin chele parvan.
Ik sansari ik bhandari ik laye deeban.
Jiv tis bhaveh tivey chalaye jiv hoveh phurman.
Oh vekhey ona nadar na aaveh bahuta eh vidan.

Aades tisey aades.
Aad aneel anad anahat jug jug eko ves. // 30 //

Wear earrings of contentment
Make labour your mantle
Smear the ashes of meditation all over
Be as pure as a virgin damsel
Carry the staff of determination.
Let your creed be equality
Conquer self to conquer the world
So melodious and yet so silent
So varied and yet the same
I am wonderstruck by the simplicity of it!

Let your food be of divine knowledge
Let your storehouse be of compassion
Let your music be of the all-pervading sound.
Creativity is the giver and the receiver
Creativity is the knower and the known
All spiritual powers are of no significance
Meeting and parting are two sides of the same coin.

So melodious and yet so silent
So varied and yet the same
I am wonderstruck by the simplicity of it!

As mythology would have it
A mother has three sons, Brahma, Vishnu, Shiva
The creator, sustainer and destroyer
Yet no one ever gets to meet the other.

So melodious and yet so silent
So varied and yet the same
I am wonderstruck by the simplicity of it!

Aasan loi loi bhandar.
Jo kichh paya so eka var.
Kar kar vekhey sirjanhar.
Nanak sache ki saachi kar.

Aades tisey aades.
Aad aneel anad anahat jug jug eko ves. // 31 //

Ikdu jeebho lakh hoi lakh hoveh lakh vees.
Lakh lakh gera aakheeyeh ek naam jagdees.
Eit rah patt pavareeya charheeye hoi ikees.
Sunn galan aakas ki keeta aayee rees.
Nanak nadri payeeye kurhi kure thees. // 32 //

Aakhan jor chupeh neh jor.
Jor na mangan dein na jor.
Jor na jeevan maran na jor.
Jor na raj maal man sor.
Jor na surati gyan vichar.
Jor na jugti chhutey sansar.
Jis hath jor kar vekhey soi.
Nanak uttam neech na koi. // 33 //

Creation is boundless and bountiful
It provides for everyone that is or will be
Creator and creativity are one
The truth is so simple and stunning

So melodious and yet so silent
So varied and yet the same
I am wonderstruck by the simplicity of it!

If I had a million tongues
And each tongue would a million times repeat
I would still not be able to say
How amazed I am at what I see.
There is a ladder reaching up to the divine
Tiny though I am, I long to climb on it.

Neither can I speak or be silent
Neither can I beg nor give
Neither can I live nor die
I have no control on anything
Neither on remembrance or forgetfulness
I know not what is the method
By which I can be liberated.
Only the Creator knows the way.

Raati rutti thiti var.
Pavan pani agni patal.
Tis vich dharti thap rakhi dharamsal.
Tis vich jee jugat ke rang.
Tin ke naam anek anant.
Karmi karmi hoi vichar.
Sacha aap sacha darbar.
Tithey sohan panch parvan.
Nadri karam pavey neesan.
Kach pakayee othey paye.
Nanak gaya japey jaye. // 34 //

Dharam khand ka eho dharam.
Gyan khand ka aakho karam.
Kete pavan pani vaisantar kete kahn mahes.
Kete barmeh gharat gharhyeeye roop rang ke ves.
Ketia karam bhumi mer kete kete dhu updes.
Kete ind chand sur kete kete mandal des.
Kete sidh budh nath kete kete devi ves.
Kete dev danav muni kete kete ratan samund.
Ketia khani ketia bani kete paat narind.
Ketia surati sewak kete Nanak ant na ant.//35//

This world is the stage
Where you perform your role
Day and night and the seasons
Air, water, fire and all elements
Are the backdrop and the props
For you to perform your part.
He is true and His abode is true
He alone can ferry you across
All else is futile struggle
It cannot bring you any closer to the truth.

The rungs of the ladder are four
The first is of observing the external
Many are the incarnations and avatars
Many are the forms in which they appear
Many obey the command and perform
Many are the gods spread across the universe
Many monsters reside along with saints
Many are the oceans full of diamonds
Many are immersed in remembrance
There is no one equal to them.

Gyan khand meh gyan parchand.
Tithey naad binod kod anand.

Saram khand ki bani roop.
Tithey gharhat gharhyeeye bahut anoop.
Ta kiya galan kaheeya na jaye.
Je ko kahe pichhey pachhtaye.
Tithey gharhyeeye surat mat man budh.
Tithey gharheeye sura sidha ki sudh. // 36 //

Karam khand ki bani jor.
Tithey hor na koi hor.
Tithey jodh mahabal sur.
Tin meh ram rahya bharpur.
Tithey seeto seeta mahima mahey.
Ta ke roop na kathney jaye.
Na oh marey na thagey jahey.
Jin ke Ram vasey man mahey.
Tithey bhagat vaseh ke lo.
Kare anand sacha man soi.

The second rung is of understanding the path
It is governed by divine knowledge

The third is of effort, struggle and service
It is the stage of translating thought into action
To mould the mind, heart and body
In tune with the divine will.
This is the state of rishis, sidhas and munis
Impossible to describe in words.

And the last stage is of dissolution
Of becoming one with the divine
It is the state of total acceptance
Of unconditional surrender
Where all duality disappears
And only one remains.
Where the immediate is the ultimate.
A state of total devotion
Where the true devotees reside
Where there is neither birth nor death.

Sachkhand vasey nirankar.
Kar kar vekhey nadar nihal.
Tithey khand mandal varbhand.
Je ko kathey ta ant na ant.
Tithey lo lo akar.

Jiv jiv hukam tivey tiv kar.
Vekhey vigsey kar vichar.
Nanak kathna karhra sar. // 37 //

Jat pahara dheeraj suniyar.
Ahran mat ved hathiyar.
Bhao khala agan tap tao.
Bhanda bhao amrit tit dhal.
Gharheeye sabad sachi taksal.
Jin ko nadar karam tin kar.
Nanak nadri nadar nihal. // 38 //

The final stage is of truth
Where the True One resides
This state of ultimate bliss is achieved
Not by knowledge and understanding alone
But by His merciful grace
It is an arduous path that has to be tread every inch
Encountering and overcoming the hurdles on the way.

Like the goldsmith puts the gold in fire
To mould it into the shape of an ornament
Likewise the mind and body
Have to be chiselled in the same fashion.
Even so, all the effort is not enough
If the divine grace is missing.
He who has the divine blessings
Sails through these stages effortlessly.

Salok

Pavan guru pani pita
mata dharat mahat.

Diwas raat doi dayee daaya
kheley sagal jagat.

Changiyaayeean buriyaayeean
vachey dharam hadur.

Karmi aapo apni
ke nere ke dur.

Jini naam dhiyaaya
gaye masakat ghal.

Nanak te mukh ujaley
keti chhuti nal. // 1 //

Salok

All creatures play in the cradle
Where air is the Guru

Water is the father, earth the mother
Day and night are the nurses.

Somewhere all the actions are recorded
The good and bad accordingly rewarded

A place is granted as per your deeds
Which may be near or far from the Creator

Those who are absorbed in Naam
They achieve the purpose of their life

They return with glowing countenances
And with them ferry many others along.

Asa-di-Var

Ek Omkar Satnam Karta Purukh Nirbhau Nirwair Akal Murat Ajooni
Saibham Gurprasad. Asa Mahalla 1.
 Var saloka naal salok bhi Mahalle Pehle ke likhey Tundey Asrajey ki
dhuni.

Salok M. 1
Balihari gur aapne diohari sadd var.
Jin manas te devte kiye karat na lagi var 1

Mahalla 2
Je sau chanda ugvey suraj charey hajar.
Etey chanan hondiyan guru bin ghor andhar. 2

M. 1
Nanak guru na chetni mann aapne suchet.
Chhutey til buaar jiu sunjey andar khet.
Khetey andar chhutia kaho Nanak sau nah.
Phaliye phuliye bapurey bhi tan vich suaah. 3

Pauri
Aapi ne aap sajio aapi ne rachiyo nao.
Duyee kudrat saajiye kar aasan ditho chao.
Data karta aap tu tus devey kare pasao.
Tu janaoi sabhse de leisei jind kavao.
Kar aasan ditho chao. // 1 //

Ek Omkar Satnam Karta Purukh Nirbhau Nirvair Akal Murat Ajooni Saibham Gurprasad.
Asa Mahalla 1, Tundey Asrajey ki Dhuni

Salok Mahalla 1
Let me surrender to my Guru
Every moment of the day, month and year.
My Guru has turned humans into gods
And he didn't take a moment to work the miracle.

Mahalla 2
Not a hundred moons and a thousand suns
Can dispel the darkness without the Guru.

Mahalla 1
Remembrance leads to full consciousness.
Without it we are hollow and useless
Like the weeds in a sesame field
Ignored and untouched by the Reaper.
Growing in a stunted manner.

Pauri
You are the Creator of this world
You have created the order that prevails
You have created nature
From where you monitor this world.
You give understanding to those with whom you are happy

Salok M 1
Sachey tere khand sachey brahmand.
Sachey tere lo sachey akar.
Sachey tere karney sarab bichar.
Sacha tera amar sacha deeban.
Sacha tera hukam sacha phurman.
Sacha tera karam sacha neesan.
Sachey tudh aakhey lakh crore.
Sachey sabh taan sachey sabh jor.
Sachi teri sifat sachi salah.
Sachi teri kudrat sachey patsah.
Nanak sach dhiyayan sach.
Jo mar jammey so kach nikach. 1

M. 1
Vadi vadiyayee ja vada nao.
Vadi vadiyayee ja sach niao.
Vadi vadiyayee ja nehchal thao.
Vadi vadiyayee janey alao.
Vadi vadiyayee bujhey sabh bhao.
Vadi vadiyayee ja puchh na jaat.
Vadi vadiyayee ja aape aap.
Nanak kaar na kathni jaye.
Keeta karna sarab rajaye. 2

Salok Mahalla 1
Your creation is true
All the worlds are true.
All the forms are true
All the thoughts are true
All the feelings are true.
Your court is true
Your order is true
Your actions are true
Your consequences are true.
Your worshippers are true
Your praises are true
My true lord, your nature is true.
Those who remember you are true
Others just come and go.

Mahalla 1
You are great and your Naam is great
You are great because you are just
You are great because you are eternal
You are great because you know all
You are great because you hear the unsaid
You are great because you give unasked
You are great because you are everywhere.
I have no words to describe you
You are all in all and everywhere.

108

Mahalla 2
Eh jag sachey ki hai kothri sachey ka vich vas.
Ikna hukam samaye lei ikna hukmey kare vinas.
Ikna bhaney kadd lei ikna maya vich niwas.
Ev bhi aakh na japyee je kisse aane ras.
Nanak gurmukh janeeye ja ko aap kare pargas. 3

Pauri
Nanak jee upaye ke likh navey dharam bahaliya.
Othey sachey hi sach nibarey chunn vakh kaddey jajmaliya.
Thao na payeyan kuriyar muh kale dojak chaliya.
Likh navey dharam bahaliya. // 2 //

Salok Mahalla 2
This world is the abode of the True One
In which some obey the Will while others don't
The former are ferried across, others are not.
No one knows who will win the divine favour.
They are your favourites whom you bless.

Pauri
You have created all living beings
You have made Dharam Rai the judge
Only the true are forgiven
The others are thrown out.
They find no place here
And are punished in hell.
Remembrance is the key to win
Forgetting leads to miserable defeat.

Salok Mahalla 1
Vismad naad vismad ved.
Vismad jee vismad bhed.
Vismad roop vismad rang.
Vismad nagey phirey jant.
Vismad pavan vismad pani.
Vismad agni khedey vidani.
Vismad dharti vismad khani.
Vismad saad lagey prani.
Vismad sanjog vismad viyag.
Vismad bhukh vismad bhog.
Vismad sifat vismad salah.
Vismad ujhar vismad rah.
Vismad nerey vismad door.
Vismad dekhey hajra hajoor.
Vekh vidan rahya vismad.
Nanak bujhan poorey bhag. 1

M. 1
Kudrat disey kudrat suniye kudrat bhao sukhsar.
Kudrat patali akasi kudrat sarab akar.
Kudrat ved puran kateba kudrat sarab vichar.
Kudrat khana pina pehnan kudrat sarab pyar.
Kudrat jaati jinsi rangi kudrat jee jahan.
Kudrat nekiya kudrat badiya kudrat maan abhiman.
Kudrat pavan pani baisantar kudrat dharti khak.
Nanak hukmey andar vekhey vartai tako tak. 2

Salok Mahalla 1
The sound is wonderful and so are the Vedas
The forms are wonderful and so are the colours.
The air is wonderful and so is water.
The fire is wonderful that plays a myriad games.

The earth is wonderful and so are all its bounties.
Human beings are wonderful with all their idiosyncrasies.
Meetings are wonderful and so are partings.

Appetite is wonderful and so is satiation.
Prayers are wonderful and so are those who pray.
Everything in your creation is wonderful.
Nanak says: Blessed are those that can see it.

Mahalla 1
You are seeing through all eyes
You are listening through all ears
You are in all the three worlds
You are in the Vedas and the Puranas.
You are eating through all mouths
You are dressing all the forms.
You are in all beings and things
You are in the virtues and the vices
You are in respect and in insult as well.
You are in everything
You make everything pure
By your sheer presence.

112

Pauri

Aapine bhog bhog ke hoi bhasmar bhaur sidhaya.
Vada hoa dunidar gal sangal ghat chalaya.
Agey karni keerat vacheeye beh lekha kar samjhaya.
Thao na hovee paudiyee hun suniye kya ruaaya.
Mann andhey janam gavaya. // 3 //

Salok Mahalla 1

Bhay vich pavan vahey sadd vao.
Bhay vich chaley lakh dariao.
Bhay vich agan kaddey vegar.
Bhay vich dharti dabbi bhar.
Bhay vich raja dharam dwar.
Bhay vich suraj bhay vich chand.
Koh karori ant na ant.
Bhay vich sidh budh sur nath.
Bhay vich adaney akas.
Bhay vich jodh mahabal sur.
Bhay vich aavey javey pur.
Sagaliya bhao likhya sir lekh.
Nanak nirbhau nirankar sach ek. 1

Pauri

People live through the body which is left behind
Even the greatest men are taken away by death
Then they are judged according to their deeds
If life has not been lived well
It is too late to repent and make amends.

Salok Mahalla 1

Your order makes the air move
Your order makes the rivers run
Your order makes the fire burn
Your order makes the earth bear the burden
Your order makes the clouds float
Your order makes the kings function
Your order makes the suns and moons move
Your order makes the gods and the wise men
Your order makes the vast sky
Your order makes the warriors and the soldiers
Your order makes them come and go.
Everything is as per your order
Only you are above your order

M. 2

Nanak nirbhau nirankar hor kete Ram Raval.
Ketia kann kahaniya kete bed bichar.
Kete nachey mangatey girh murh purey tal.
Bajari bajar meh aaye kaddey bajar.
Gavey rajey raniya boleh aal pataal.
Lakh takiya ke mundre lakh takiya ke haar.
Jit tan payeeye Nanaka se tan hoveh chhar.
Gyan na galli dhundheeye kathna karrha sar.
Karam miley ta payeeye hor hikmat hukam khuar. 2

Pauri

Nadar kare je aapni ta nadri satgur paya.
Eh jio bahute janam bharmiya ta satgur sabad sunaya.
Satgur jevad data ko nahi sabh suniyo lok sabaya.
Satgur miliye sach paya jini vicho aap gavaya.
Jin sacho sach bujhaya. // 4 //

Mahalla 2

You are the true formless one
All others are your various forms.
Many are the Vedas and the Mahabharatas
Many dancers dance to different tunes
Many kings and queens speak incoherently
Many are engrossed in making money
Many are busy acquiring knowledge
But knowledge is not found in words
True knowledge is a blessing from above.

Pauri

With your grace the Guru is found
After seeking and searching for many lives.
The Satguru is the greatest giver
Let this be understood by all.
The Guru alone can dissolve the ego
And give an insight into the truth.

Salok Mahalla 1
Ghariya sabhey gopiya pahar kann gopal.
Gahaney pavan pani baisantar chand suraj avtar.
Sagali dharti maal dhan vartan sarab janjal.
Nanak musey gyan vihuni khaye gaya jamkal. 1

M. 1
Vayen cheley nachan gur.
Paer hilayan pheran sir.
Ud ud rava jhatey paye.
Vekhey lok hasey ghar jaye.
Rotiya kaaran purey tal.
Aap pachharey dharti nal.
Gavan gopiya gavan kaan.
Gavan Seeta Raje Ram.
Nirbhau nirankar sach nam.
Ja ka kiya sagal jahan.
Sewak seweh karam charao.
Bhini raen jina man chao.
Sikhi sikhya gur vichar.
Nadri karam langhaye par.
Kolu charkha chakki chak.
Thal viroley bahut anant.
Latu madhaniya angah.
Pankhi bhaudiya laen na sah.
Suuye charh bhavayeeye jant.
Nanak bhaundya ganat na ant.

Salok Mahalla 1

The hours are the Gopis
The quarters of the day Krishna
Air, water and fire are the ornaments
The sun and moon are his incarnations
The entire vegetation is the backdrop.
In this enchanting drama
The world is being robbed by death.

Mahalla 1

The followers play the instruments
The leaders dance to their tunes
They tap their feet and bang their heads
All they get is dust in their hair
People laugh at them because
They are doing this for the sake of food.
Their dance is only tiring them
Beating the ground underneath.
They sing as Gopis and Krishna
They sing as Ram and Sita.
They go round and round in circles
Moving in their respective cages
They reach nowhere.
They churn vigorously in water
All their efforts go waste
Sometimes they laugh as they dance
And then they leave crying.
There is no end to this play of shadows

Bandhan bandh bhavaye soi.
Payeye kirat nachey sabh koi.
Nach nach haseh chaley se roi.
Ud na jahi sidh na hoi.
Nachan kuddan man ka chao.
Nanak jin man bhou tina man bhao. 2

Pauri
Nao tera nirankar hai naye leyeeye narak na jayeeye.
Jio pind sabh tis da de khajey aakh sunayeeye.
Je lorheye changa aapna kar punnu neech sadayeeye.
Je jarvana parharey jar ves karedi aayeeye.
Ko rahey na bhariye payeeye. // 5 //

They are caught in their own traps
Each one is dancing his own dance
As has been ordained.
But it leads nowhere.
All this activity is mere recreation.
Those who love need not do anything;
They have already arrived.

Pauri
Remembering you there is no hell
All that we have is yours
Let us give and forget about it
Or else giving is of no use.
Doing good to others and being humble
Is the only way to root out the fear of death.
And when the time comes we will go in peace.

Salok Mahalla 1

Musalmana sifat sariyat parh parh kareh bichar.
Bande se je paveh vich bandi vekhan ko didar.
Hindu salahi salahan darsan roop apar.
Teerath naveh archa puja agar vas bahkar.
Jogi sunn dhyavan jete alakh nam kartar.
Sukham murat naam niranjan kaya ka akar.
Satiya man santokh upajey dene ko vichar.
De de mangeh sahsa guna sobh kare sansar.
Chora jara te kuriyara kharaba vekar.
Ik honda khaye chaleh aithao tina bhi kayee kar.
Jal thal jiya puriya loa akara akar.
Oye je aakheh so tu hai janeh tina bhi teri sar.
Nanak bhagata bhukh salahan sach nam adhar.
Sada anand raheh din rati gunvantiya pa chhar. 1

M. 1

Mitti musalman ki perhey payee kumiyar.
Gharh bhandey itta kiya jaldi kare pukar.
Jal jal rovey bapuri jharh jharh pavey angiyar.
Nanak jin karte kaaran kiya so janey kartar.

Pauri

Bin satgur kiney na payo bin satgur kiney na paya.
Satgur vich aap rakhiyon kar pargat aakh sunaya.
Satgur miliye sada mukat hai jin vicho moh chukaya.
Uttam eh vichar hai jin sachey sio chit laya.
Jagjeevan data paya. // 6 //

Salok Mahalla 1

The Muslims read the Quran and contemplate it
The Hindus worship idols and go on pilgrimages
The Yogis go to the wilderness and meditate
On that which is formless and has taken shape.
The Satis give up the desire to live
The philanthropists give but seek rewards.
The thieves commit sin and rot in hell.
They squander their wealth and return empty handed
You know what is happening in all the worlds.
The devotees are thirsty of your presence
They are humble and truly blessed.

Mahalla 1

The corpse of a Muslim decomposes
The dust may then become part of the clay
With which the potter makes pots
And puts them in the furnace to set.
Only the Creator knows the scheme of things.

Pauri

No one has discovered the truth without the Guru.
It is because the Creator is manifest in the Guru.
With the Guru's grace we can be free
So let us just love the Guru and forget all else
He is the only link with the Creator of the universe.

Salok Mahalla 1
Hau vich aya hau vich gaya.
Hau vich jammya hau vich mua.
Hau vich ditta hau vich laya.
Hau vich khatiya hau vich gaya.
Hau vich sachiyar hau vich kuriyar.
Hau vich paap punn vichar.
Hau vich narak surag avtar.
Hau vich haseh hau vich rovey.
Hau vich bhariye hau vich dhovey.
Hau vich jaati jinsi khovey.
Hau vich murakh hau vich siyana.
Mokh mukat ki sar na jana.
Hau vich maya hau vich chhaya.
Haumey kar kar jant upaya..
Haumey bujhey ta dar sujhey.
Gyan vihuna kath kath lujhey.
Nanak hukmi likhiye lekh.
Jeha vekhey teha vekh. 1

Mahalla 2
Haumey eha jaat hai haumey karam kamahe.
Haumey eyee bandhna phir phir joni pahe.
Haumey kitho upajey kit sanjam eh jaye.
Haumey eho hukam hai payeeye kirat phirahe.
Haumey deerag rog hai daru bhi iss mahe.
Kirpa kare je aapni ta gur ka sabad kamahe.
Nanak kahe suno jano it sanjam dukh jahe. 2

Salok Mahalla 1

We exist because of our individual ego
We are born and we die as individuals
We give and take as individuals
We earn and spend as individuals
We are good or bad as separate egos
We laugh and cry as individual egos
We are foolish or intelligent as egos.
The entire gambit of maya is of the ego
Ego is the source of all individual forms.

So, we need to understand this ego.
Without understanding we argue unnecessarily.
Nanak says: Try and understand the divine order
Look deep into things as they are.

Mahalla 2

The ego is a disease but its remedy is in it only
The cycle of birth and death is because of the ego
All our actions are dictated by our ego.
Ego is the cage in which we are imprisoned.
We don't know where ego comes from
Nor do we know how to get rid of it.
The malady carries its remedy in its bosom.
Understanding the ego leads the way out of it.
With the grace of the Guru it can be dissolved
This is the only way; there is none other.

124

Pauri

Sev kiti santokhyee jini sacho sach dhiyaya.

Oni mandey paer na rakhiyo kar sukrit dharam kamaya.

Oni duniya torhey bandhna ann pani thorha khaya.

Tu bakhsisi agla nit deveh charheh sawaya.

Vadiyayee vada paya. // 7 //

Pauri

Those who serve with a devoted heart
Will do no wrong in their life.
Following the right path
They break the shackles of this world
Living a disciplined life
They prepare for a comfortable departure.
They win the favour of the Creator.

Salok Mahalla 1
Purkhan birkhan teerathan tattan meghan khetanh.
Deepan loaan mandalan khandan varbhandanh.
Andaj jeraj utbhujan khani setajanh.
So mit janey Nanaka saran meran jantanh.
Nanak jant upaye ke sammaley sabhnah.
Jin karte karna kiya chinta bhi karni tah.
So karta chinta kare jin upaya jag.
Tis johari suasat tis tis deeban abhag.
Nanak sachey naam bin kya tikka kya tag. 1

M. 1
Lakh nekia changiyayeeya lakh punna parvan.
Lakh tap upar teeratha sahaj jog beban.
Lakh surtan sangram rann meh chhutey pran.
Lakh surati lakh gyan dhyan parhiyeeye path puran.
Jin karte karna kiya likhya aavan jan.
Nanak mati mithiya karm sacha neesan. 2

Pauri
Sacha sahib ek tu jin sacho sach vartaya.
Jis tu de tis miley sach ta tini sach kamaya.
Satgur miliye sach paya jinke hirday sach vasaya.
Murakh sach na janni manmukhi janam gavaya.
Vich duniya kahe aaya. // 8 //

Salok Mahalla 1
In the human beings, trees, holy places, clouds and fields
In the creation from eggs, womb, seeds and other means
He resides in all the living beings
In the seas, forests and mountains
He has created them and sustains them
He takes care of all His Creation.

Have faith in His scheme of things
That is the best prayer.
All else is a hollow display of religiosity.

Mahalla 1
Millions of good deeds or charities
Millions of pilgrimages or austerities
Millions of battles fought in battlefields
Millions of attempts to meditate
Millions of recitations of holy books
Cannot erase the fate destined for each one.

Pauri
There is only one Creator
His creation is as true as Him.
But, we will realise this truth
Only with the grace of the Guru.
The Guru will fill the heart with devotion
Others are too full of themselves
They waste this precious opportunity
Of being born as human beings.

128

Salok Mahalla 1
Parh parh gadi ladiye parh parh bhariye sath.
Parh parh berhi payeeye parh parh gadiye khat.
Parheeye jete baras baras parheeye jete mas.
Parheeye jeti aarja parheeye jete sas.
Nanak lekhey ik gal hor haumey jhakna jhakh. 1

M. 1
Likh likh parhya. Teta karhya.
Bahu teerath bhavya. Teto lavya.
Bahu bhekh kiya. Dehi dukh diya.
Sauh ve jia apna kiya.
Ann na khaya saad gavaya.
Bahu dukh paya duja bhaya.
Bastra na pehrey. Ahnis kehrey.
Mon viguta. Kyu jagey gur bin suta.
Pag upetana. Apna kiya kamana.
Al mal khayee sir chhayee payee.
Murakh andhey patt gavayee.
Vin navey kichh thaye na payee.
Rahe bebani marhi masani.
Andh na janey phir pachhtani.
Satgur bhetey so sukh paye.
Har ka naam man vasaye.
Nanak nadar kare so paye.
Aas andesey te nehkewal haumey sabad jalaye. 2

Salok Mahalla 1
Even if we read a cartload of books
Even if we read for months and years
Even if we read as long as we live
There is only one thing to learn
All else is senseless jargon.

Mahalla 1
It only strengthens our ego
If we read all that is written
If we go to all the pilgrimages
If we perform all the rituals
We only subject the body to pain
If we fast we suffer from hunger
If we shed clothes we gain nothing
If we vow not to speak it hardly matters
Because without the Guru we cannot awaken.
Whatever we do comes back to us in many ways
Starving the body only spoils our health
Why not follow the Guru instead
And let him lead us out of this mess.
Living in isolated places or in graveyards
We only torture ourselves
Instead if we go to the Guru
We will find the true path and reach someday
The Guru will burn our ego and dissolve all doubts.

Pauri

Bhagat tere man bhavdey dar sohan keerat gavdey.
Nanak karma bahrey dar dho na lehni dhavdey.
Ik mool na bujhan aapna anhonda aap ganayndey..
Hau dhadhi ka neech jaat hor uttam jaat sadayedey.
Tin manga je tujhey dhyayendey. // 9 //

Salok Mahalla 1

Koorh raja koorh parja koorh sabh sansar.
Koorh mandap koorh marhi koorh baisanhar.
Koorh soina koorh rupa koorh pehnanhar.
Koorh kaya koorh kaparh koorh roop apar.
Koorh miya koorh bibi khap hoi khar.
Koorh koorhe neho laga visriya kartar.
Kis nal kije dosti sabh jag chalanhar.
Koorh mitha koorh makhiyo koorh dobey poor.
Nanak vakhaney benati tudh bajh koorho koorh. 1

M. 1

Sach ta par janeeye ja ridey sacha hoi.
Koorh ki mal uttarey tan kare hachha dhoi.
Sach ta par janeeye ja sach dharey pyar.
Nao sunn man rehseeye ta paye mokh dwar.

Pauri

Your devotees sing your praises day and night
The others find no solace and wander aimlessly.
They do not know who they are
And spend a lifetime in illusions.
I am the humble servant
The others claim to be superior
I seek those that remember you always.

Salok Mahalla 1

Everything visible is false
The kings, the subjects and the entire world are false
False are gold, silver and those who wear them.
False are the bodies and the dresses that adorn them.
The husband is false and so is the wife
Everyone is in love with the false
They have forgotten the only one that is true.
Whom should we befriend when everything is false?
Nanak says: Without thee everything is false.

Mahalla 1

We can know the truth if our heart is pure
If we remove the layers of falsehood from it
If we keep our body and mind clean.
If we love the only one that is true
By listening to his sound we will find the way.

Sach ta par janeeye ja jugat janey jio.
Dharat kaya saadh ke vich dei karta bio.
Sach ta par janeeye ja sikh sachi lei.
Daya janey jee ki kichh punn daan karei.
Sach ta par janeeye ja atam teerath kare niwas.
Satguru nu puchh ke beh rahe kare niwas.
Sach sabhna hoi daru paap kaddey dhoi.
Nanak vakhaney benati jin sach palley hoi. 2

Pauri
Daan mahinda tali khak je mile ta mastak layeeye.
Koorha lalach chhadiye ik man hoi ik dhiyayeeye.
Phal teveho payeeye jevehi kaar kamayeeye.
Je hovey purab likhya ta dhoor tina di payeeye.
Matt thorhi sev gavayeeye. // 10 //

Salok Mahalla 1
Sach kaal koorh vartiya kal kalakh betal.
Bio beej patt lei gaye ab kyu ugavey dal.
Je ik hoi ta ugavey rutti hu rutt hoi.
Nanak pahe bahra korey rang na soi.
Bhay vich khumbh charhayeeye saram pah tan hoi.
Nanak bhagati je rapey koorhe soi na koi. 1

We will know the true one if we know the way
If we sow the seed of love in the field of the heart
If we are compassionate towards others
If our soul resides in the pilgrimage of love
With the help and guidance of the Guru
We will know the true one.
Truth is the remedy of all sins and sorrows.

Pauri
If I can get the dust of your feet
I will smear my forehead with it.
I will give up the false and remember the true one
I will get to this state only if I have walked this way
By serving the Guru I dissolve the ego
And come closer to the truth.

Salok Mahalla 1
Truth has become rare while falsehood prevails
Then how can we expect the crop to grow
After we have removed the cover from the seed?
A moth-ridden seed is of no use.
Just as a cloth cannot be dyed unless it is wet
The heart devoid of love cannot find the truth.
The heart has to be dyed with love and devotion
Only then it can wash away the false layers.

M. 1

Lab paap doi raja mehta koorh hoya sikdar.
Kam neb sadd puchheeye beh beh kare bichar.
Andhi raiyat gyan vihuni bhahe bharey murdar.
Gyani nacheh vaje vaveh roop kareh sigar.
Uchey kukeh vada gaveh jodha ka vichar.
Murakh pundit hikmat hujjat sanjay kareh pyar.
Dharmi dharam kareh gavaveh mangeh mokh dwar.
Jati sadaye jugat na janey chhadd bahe ghar bar.
Sabh ko pura aape hovey ghat na koi aakhey.
Patt parvana pichhey payeeye ta Nanak toliya japey. 2

M. 1

Vadi so vajag Nanaka sacha vekhey soi.
Sabhni chhala mariya karta kare so hoi.
Agey jaat na jor hai agey jio navey.
Jin ki lekhey patt pavey changey sei ke.

Pauri

Dhur karam jina ko tudh paya ta tini khasam dhiyaya.
Ena janta ke vass kichh nahi tudh veki jagat upaya.
Ikna no tu mel lehe ik aapoh tudh khuaya.
Gur kirpa te janiya jithey tudh aap bujhaya.
Sahajey hi sach samaya. // 11 //

Mahalla 1
Sin is the king; greed his minister
And falsehood the constable
Lust is the consultant
The subjects are blind in ignorance
Seething in the fire of desire.
The intellectuals dance a different tune
The beautiful are busy adorning themselves
They are drowned in their own noises
The foolish and wise alike are deluded
The religious person is as deluded as them
Because he desires salvation for his efforts
But the desire turns the efforts to naught.
The yogi has not found the secret
He renounces his home in search of it.
Everyone believes he is doing the right thing
But only He knows who will succeed ultimately.

M. 1
Only He knows what is right or wrong
All the others are trying and learning
In His court neither caste nor strength are the criteria
Only those who are accepted have arrived.

Pauri
We can remember you only with your blessings
We are utterly helpless
You let some of us come close
While you keep others away
I know this with the help of the Guru
The Guru makes knowing possible for me.

Salok Mahalla 1
Dukh daru sukh rog bhaya ja sukh taam na hoyee.
Tu karta karna main nahi ja hau kari na hoyee. 1
Balihari kudrat vasya.
Tera ant na jayee lakhya. 1 Rahao.
Jaat meh jot jot meh jaata akal kala bharpur rahya.
Tu sacha sahib sifat suaaliya jin kiti so par paya.
Kaho Nanak kartey kiya bata jo kichh karna so kar rahya. 2

M. 2
Jog sabdan gyan sabdan bed sabdan brahmaneh.
Khatri sabdan sur sabdan sudra sabdan prakriteh.
Sarab sabdan ek sabdan je ko janey bheo.
Nanak ta ka das hai soyee niranjan deo. 3

M. 2
Ek krisnan sarab deva dev deva ta atma.
Atma basdevas je ko janey bheo.
Nanak ta ka das hai soyee niranjan deo. 4

Salok Mahalla 1
Pain is the remedy; pleasure is pain
The pleasure which takes me away from you.
You are the life force in me
Without you I cannot do anything.
You are living in every being.
I cannot fathom you.
You are the light in every being
And in your light is everything.
You permeate the entire creation.
We can ferry across by realising you.
By admiring and marvelling at your creation.

Mahalla 2
The all-pervasive sound is the yoga
It is the path of knowledge as well.
The Brahmins follow the path of knowledge
The Kshatriyas follow the path of valour
The Shudras follow the path of service
But the sound leads to the divine
Nanak follows that formless divinity.

Mahalla 2
The spirit of all gods is in Krishna
The same spirit that pervades in the creation
Nanak follows that formless divinity.

M. 1

Kumbhey badha jal rahey jal bin kumbh na hoi.
Gyan ka badha man rahey gur bin gyan na hoi. 5

Pauri

Parhya hovey gunahgar ta omi saadh na mareeye.
Jeha ghaley ghalna teveho nao pachareeye.
Aisee kala na khediye jit dargah gaya hareeye.
Parhya atey omiya vichar agey vichareeye.
Muh chale so agey mareeye. // 12 //

Mahalla 1
Just as water is contained in the pitcher
But there is no pitcher without the water.
Similarly, knowledge is contained in the mind
But there is no knowledge without the Guru.

Pauri
In the divine court, justice will be done
The learned and illiterate will be treated alike
They will be judged according to their deeds
The learned will not be forgiven for his learning
The illiterate will get preference if his deeds are good.
Therefore, don't indulge in activities
That will make you lose the game ultimately.

Salok Mahalla 1
Nanak meru sarir ka ik rath ik rathvah.
Jug jug pher vatayeeye gyani bujheh tahe.
Satjug rath santokh ka dharam agey rathvahu.
Tretai rath jatey ka jor agey rathvahu.
Dwapar rath tapey ka sat agey rathvahu.
Kaljug rath agan ka koorh agey rathvahu. 1

M. 1
Sam kahe setambar swami sach meh aachhey sach samavey.
Rig kahe rahya bharpur. Ram nam deva meh sur.
Naai laye parachhat jahe. Nanak toh mokhantar pahe.
Juj meh jor chhali chandravan kaan krisan jadam bhaya.
Parjat gopi lei aya brindaban meh rang kiya.
Kal meh bed athrban hua nao khudayee allah bhaya.
Neel bastra lei kaprey pehrey turak pathani amal kiya.
Charey bed hoye sachyar. Parhey gunneh tin char vichar.
Bhao bhagat kar neech sadaye. Toh Nanak mokhantar paye. 2

Pauri
Satgur vitoh varya jit miliye khasam samalya.
Jin kar updes gyan anjan diya eni netri jagat nihalya.
Khasam chhod dujey lagey dubbey se vanjarya.
Satguru hai bohitha virley kiney vicharya.
Kar kirpa paar utarya. // 13 //

Salok Mahalla 1

The master of the body is the soul
It is like the driver of the carriage
In Satyug, the carriage of contentment was driven by religion
In Traita, the carriage of yoga was driven by discipline
In Dwapar, the carriage of tapa was driven by truth
In Kalyug, the carriage of desire is driven by falsehood.

Mahalla 1

The Samveda talks of white as purity
When everyone lived pure lives
The Rigveda talks of the reign of Ram
When his presence turned sinners to saints.
The Yajurveda talks of Krishna's reign
When people danced in sheer bliss.
The Atharvaveda talks of the Turks
When the lord was called Allah.
All the four Vedas speak the truth of their times.
Nanak says: Be humble and attain moksha.

Pauri

The Guru reminds us of the Creator
He helps us see Him everywhere
Without the Guru there is no way.
He is the boat to ferry us across this ocean
But only a few realise this fact.

Salok Mahalla 1
Simmal rukh sarayra ati deeragh ati much.
Oye je aavey aas kar jaye nirasey kit.
Phal phikey phul bakbakey kamm na aavey pat.
Mithat neevee Nanaka gunn changiyayeean tat.
Sabh ko nivey aap ko par ko nivey na koi.
Dhar taraju toliye nivey so goura hoi.
Apradhi duna niveh jo hanta mirgahe.
Sis nivayeeye kya thiye ja ridey kasudhey jahe. 1

M. 1
Parh pustak sandhya badan.
Sil pujas bagal samadhan.
Mukh jhooth bibhukhan saran.
Traipal tihal bicharan.
Gal mala tilak lilatan.
Doi dhoti bastra kapatan.
Je janas brahman karman.
Sabh phokat nehcho karman.
Kaho Nanak nehcho dhiyavey.
Vin satgur vaat na pavey. 2

Pauri
Kaparh roop suhavna chhadd duniya andar javna.
Manda changa aapna aape hi kita pavna.
Hukam kiye mann bhavdey rah bheerhe agey javna.
Nanga dojak chaliya ta disey khara daravna.
Kar augan pachhotavna // 14 //

Salok Mahalla 1

The simal tree is very tall and broad
But it has nothing to give;
Its flowers and fruits are tasteless
And it has no leaves to give shade.
Nanak says: Humility is the mother of all virtues.
But everyone bends for himself
No one bends for the sake of others.
In a scale the lower is the heavier
But the sinner bends double like the hunter chasing the deer.
Bowing the head is useless
If there is pride in the heart.

M. 1

Reading the holy books
Or worshipping the idols
Repeating the mantras
Or sitting in the lotus posture
Wearing the tilak and mala
Or knowing all the rituals
All are useless activities.
Just remember the divine lord
With the guidance of the Guru.

Pauri

When death happens we will leave everything behind
Including the beautiful body and the fancy clothes.
We will take with us the account of our deeds
The path ahead is very narrow
We will stand naked in the divine court
We will look scary because of our sins.

Salok Mahalla 1

Daya kapah santokh soot jat gandi sat vatt.
Ehu janeo jee ka hayee ta pande ghatt.
Na eh tuttey na mal lagey na eh jale na jaye.
Dhan so manas Nanaka jo gal chale paye.
Chaukarh mul anaya beh chowke paya.
Sikha kann charhayeean gur brahman thiya.
Oh mua oh jharh paya vetaga gaya. 1

M. 1

Lakh choriyan lakh jariyan lakh koorhiyan lakh gaal.
Lakh thagiyan pehnamiyan raat dinas jee naal.
Tag kapahu kattiye brahman vattey aaye.
Kuh bakra rinn khaya sabh ko aakhey paye.
Hoi purana suttiyeeye bhi phir payeeye hor.
Nanak tag na tuttyee je tag hovey jor. 2

M. 1

Naaye manniye patt upajey salahi sach soot.
Dargah andar payeeye tag na tutas poot. 3

Salok Mahalla 1
Let compassion be the cotton
Let contentment be the thread
Let discipline be the twist
O Pundit! If you have such a janeo,
Give it to me
It will neither break nor get dirty
It will neither get wet or burnt.
Blessed is the man who will wear it.
Without it all the rituals are hollow.
Whether they are of purifying the kitchen
Or whispering the mantra in the ear.
Because the janeo will be burnt in the pyre
And the Brahmin will have to go alone.

Mahalla 1
After wearing the janeo people go about
Committing various kinds of sins.
The thread is made of cotton
It is twisted by a Brahmin
There is a feast to celebrate the ceremony.
When it wears out it is thrown
And it is replaced by another one.
If the thread was strong would it break?

Mahalla 1
Let acceptance of Thy Will be the cotton
Let remembrance be the twist.
Make a janeo of such a thread
This thread will stay for ever.

146

M. 1
Tag na indri tag na nari.
Bhalke thuk paveh nit daarhi.
Tag na paeri tag na hathi.
Tag na jehva tag na akhi.
Vetaga aape vattey.
Vatt dhagey avra ghattey.
Lei bharh kare viaahu.
Kadd kagal dasey rahu.
Sunn vekho loka eh vidan.
Man andha nao sujan.

Pauri
Sahib hoi dayal kirpa kare ta sai kar karayesi.
So sewak sewa kare jisno hukam manayesi.
Hukam manniye hovey parvan ta khasmey ka mahal payesi.
Khasmey bhaveh so kare manuh chindya so phal payesi.
Ta dargah paindha jayesi. // 15 //

Salok Mahalla 1
Gaoo birahman ko kar lavuh gobar karan na jayee.
Dhoti tikka te japmali dhaan malechha khayee.
Antar puja parhe kateba sanjam turka bhai.
Chhodile pakhanda. Nam layeeye jahe taranda. 1

Mahalla 1

The sacred thread is not given to women.
Nor does it curb the desires of the senses.
There is none for hands and feet
Nor for the eyes and tongue
It is twisted like any other thread
Then what makes it sacred?
It hardly serves any purpose except perhaps
It deludes you into thinking you are great.

Pauri

With the divine grace everything is done.
He who accepts Thy Will serves with dedication.
Such a person finds place in the divine court.
And he gets what he seeks.
He finds a place in the divine court.

Salok Mahalla 1

The cow or cow dung cannot purify us
The tilak or the rosary is not enough
Reading of holy texts will get us nowhere
So, give up all pretence
And follow the true one.

148

M. 1

Manas khaney kare niwaj.
Chhuri vagayan tin gal taag.
Tin ghar brahman pureh naad.
Ona bhi aaveh ohi saad.
Koorhi ras koorha vapar.
Koorh bol kare ahar.
Saram dharam ka dera dur.
Nanak koorh rahya bharpur.
Mathey tikka terh dhoti kakhayee.
Hath chhuri jagat kasayee.
Neel bastra peher hoveh parvan.
Malechh dhaan lei pujeh puran.
Abhakhya ka kutha bakra khana.
Chowkey upar kisey na jana.
De ke chowka kaddi kar.
Upar aaye baithey koorhiar.
Matt bhittey ve matt bhittey.
Eh ann asada bhittey.
Tan phittey pherh karen .
Mann jhoothey chulli bharen.
Kaho Nanak sach dhiyayeeye.
Such haveh ta sach payeeye. 2

Pauri
Chitey andar sabh ko vekh nadri heth chalaynda.
Aape de vadiyayeeyan aape hi karam karaynda.
Vaddo vada vadd medni sirey sir dhandhey laiynda.
Nadar upathi je kare sultana ghah karaynda.
Dar mangan bhikh na paiynda. // 16 //

Mahalla 1
Men do all sorts of things
They argue on petty issues
The whole thing is meaningless
The priest is full of falsehood.
His words do not match with his deeds
He is ready to kill even as he counts the beads.

False is his speech and false his acts
False are the paths prescribed by the priest
False is his dress and false his rituals
He recites mantras but stabs the poor

He may dress up as a priest
But his actions speak differently.
False are the restrictions imposed by him
False are their pretensions of purity.

They talk of impurities in food
While their hearts are full of falsehood.
Only the pure at heart can be truly pure.

Pauri
The True One watches everything
He knows us from inside out
He has allotted us our tasks.
He can turn kings into beggars
If He turns his merciful gaze away.

Salok Mahalla 1

Je muhaka ghar muhey ghar muhe pitri de.
Agey vasat siyaniye pitri chor kare.
Vaddiye hath dalal ke musphi eh kare.
Nanak agey so mile je khatey ghaley de. 1

M. 1

Jio joru sir navani aaveh varo var.
Joothey jootha mukh vasey nit nit hoi khuar.
Suchey eh na aakhiye bahen je pinda dhoi.
Suchey sei Nanaka jin man vasiya soi. 2

Pauri

Turey palaney pavan veg har rangi harm sawaliya.
Kothey mandap marhiya laye baithey ghar pasariya.
Cheej karan man bhavde hari bujhan nahi hariya.
Kar phurmayis khaya vekh mahlat maran visariya.
Jar aayee joban hariya. // 17 //

Salok Mahalla 1

If a thief steals and offers it to his forefathers
It will be recognised and they will have to pay for it.
Then all of them will be punished
Because one gets the reward for one's actions.

Mahalla 1

Like a woman menstruates every month
Everyone gets polluted everyday.
We cannot become pure by bathing alone
Pure are those that are attuned to the True One.

Pauri

If we remain enchanted by
The fast horses with fancy saddles
And the magnificent mansions spread across
We must know that they are shortlived
Because youth will fade into old age very soon.

152

Salok Mahalla 1
Jekar sutak manniye sabh te sutak hoi.
Gohey atey lakri andar keerha hoi.
Jete daane ann ke jeean bajh na koi.
Sutak kyu kar rakhiye sutak pavey rasoi.
Nanak sutak ev na uttarey gyan utarey dhoi. 1

M. 1
Man ka sutak lobh hai jehva sutak koorh.
Akhi sutal vekhna par triya par dhan roop.
Kanni sutak kann pe layetbari khaye.
Nanak hansa admi badhey jumpur jaye. 2

M. 1
Sabho sutak bharam hai dujey lagey jaye.
Khana peena pavitar hai diton rijak sambahe.
Nanak jini gurmukh bujhya tina sutak nahe. 3

Pauri
Satgur vada kar salahiye jis vich vadiya vadiyayeeya.
Sah mele ta nadri aayeeya.
Ja tis bhana ta man vasayeeya.
Kar hukam mastak hath dhar vicho maar kaddiya buriyayeeya.
Sah tuthey naunidh payeeya. // 18 //

Salok Mahalla 1
If purity and pollution are big issues
Then it needs to be remembered that
Everything is impure
The firewood and cow dung have worms
Each grain of wheat has life in it
We have impurities in the kitchen
Then why pretend to make it pure.
Only understanding can remove impurities.

M. 1
The heart is polluted with greed
The tongue is polluted with lies.
The eyes are polluted with desire
For another man's woman and wealth.
The ears are polluted with backbiting.
These are the shackles that bind man down.

M. 1
The biggest pollution is doubt
It leads us astray.
Know that life and death are His Will
Eating and drinking is pure
Because it sustains us.
Nanak says: He who accepts His Will
Need not worry about what is pure
And what is not.

Pauri
The Guru has the power to unite us with the lord
His hand on our head will wash all our sins away.
And we will attain the ultimate freedom.

Salok Mahalla 1
Pehla sucha aap hoi suchey baitha aaye.
Suchey agey rakhion koi na bhitiyo jaye.
Sucha hoi ke jehwiya laga parhan salok.
Kuhathi jayee satiya kis eh laga dokh.
Ann devta pani devta baisantar devta loon.
Panjva paya ghirat. Ta hoya pak pavit.
Papi sio tan gadiya thuka payeeya tit.
Jit mukh naam na ucharey bin navey ras khaye.
Nanak evey janeeye tit mukh thuka paye. 1

M. 1.
Bhand nimmiye bhand jammiye bhand mangan viaahu.
Bhanduh hovey dosti bhanduh chale rahu.
Bhand mua bhand bhaliye bhand hovey bandhan.
So kyu manda aakhiye jit jammey rajan.
Bhanduh hi bhand upajey bhandey bajh na koi.
Nanak bhandey bahra eko sacha soi.
Jit mukh sada salahiye bhaga rati char.
Nanak te mukh ujaley tit sachey darbar. 2

Salok Mahalla 1
Observe the Brahmin cook in the kitchen
First he washes and bathes
Then he sits on a purified place
Then he repeats the mantra
While he prepares pure food
He takes all precautions to keep it pure
Then how did it become impure?
Because it is made by a sinner
Sinner is he who forgets the lord.
He concentrates on food forgetting the giver.
Such food is worse than filth.

M. 1
We are conceived and born by woman
We grow up and marry a woman
Woman is our friend and guide
If one woman dies we look for another
Woman carries the world forward
Then why consider her inferior?
She is the mother of the kings
Woman is the mother of woman
Without woman there is nothing.
Only the True One is above woman.
Remembrance is the only way out
Remembering the Creator we will find the way.

156

Pauri

Sabh ko aakhey aapna jis nahi so chun kaddiye.
Kita payeeye aapna aape hi lekha sandiye.
Ja rahna nahi eit jag kayit garab handiye.
Manda kise na aakhiye parh akhar ehu bujhiye.
Moorkhey naal na lujhiye. // 19 //

Salok Mahalla 1

Nanak phikey boliye tan man phika hoi.
Phiko phika sadiye phike phiki soi.
Phika dargah satiye muh thuka phike paye.
Phika murakh aakhiye pana lahe sajaye. 1

Pauri

Everyone has his own theories
No one knows who will be chosen
And who will be plucked and weeded out.
We will face the consequences of our deeds.
When we are not here to stay
Then what do we feel proud of?
There is no enemy outside
Other than the foolish mind
That plays games with us all the time.

Salok Mahalla 1

Talking sweetly is a good quality
Otherwise we become unpleasant
And will be thrown out of any company
Including the divine court.
An unpleasant person is a fool
He gets beaten for his own doing.

M. 1

Andaruh jhoothey paij bahar duniya andar phael.
Athsath teerath je navey uttarey nahi mael.
Jin patt andar bahar guddarh te bhaley sansar.
Tin nehu laga rabb seti dekhney vichar.
Rang hasey rang roveh chup bhi kar jahe.
Parvah nahi kise keri bajh sachey nah.
Dar vaat upar kharach manga jabey dei ta khahe.
Deeban eko kalam eka hama tuma mel.
Dar laye lekha peerh chhutey Nanaka jio tel. 2

Pauri

Aape hi karna kiyo kal aape hi te dhariye.
Dekhey kita aapna dhar kachi pakki sariye.
Jo aaya so chalsi sabh koi aayee variye.
Jis ke jee pran hai kyu sahib manuh visariye.
Aapan hathi aapna aape hi kaj sawariye. // 20 //

Mahalla 1
Those who are false inside
But pretend to be otherwise
They may bathe in holy waters
But cannot wash away the dirt.
Others who are clean inside
They may be wearing rags
Still they are far superior.
They love and long for the divine.
Like lovers they laugh and cry
Without bothering about public opinion.
They remain connected to the divine.
They rely on the divine will
That is their only command.
Others who think in terms of you and me
Are made to suffer like hell.

Pauri
You are the Creator of the universe
You have the power to make it work
You watch it and judge each one.
He who has come must go
Each in his own turn.
Remembrance is the key to successful living.
How can we afford to forget the lord
When His life breath keeps us alive?

Salok Mahalla 1

Eh kinehi aaski dujey lagey jaye.
Nanak aasak kandiye sad hi rahey samaye.
Changey changa kar maney mandey manda hoi.
Aasak eh na aakhiye je lekhey vartey soi. 1

Mahalla 2

Salam jawab dovey kare muddhu ghutha jaye.
Nanak dovey koorhiya thaye na kayee paye. 2

Pauri

Jit sewiye sukh payiye so sahib sada samaliye.
Jit kita payiye aapna sa ghal buri kyu ghaliye.
Manda mool na kichayee de lammi nadar nihaliye.
Jio sahib naal na hariye teveha paasa dhaliye.
Kichh laahey upar ghaliye. // 21 //

Salok Mahalla 2
This is not love that longs for the other
True lover is one who dissolves in the beloved.
This is not love that calculates give and take
This is not love that returns good for good
This is not love that returns bad for bad.

Mahalla 2
He who bows and questions at the same time
He will remain bereft of everything
Because both these actions are hollow
They will lead nowhere.

Pauri
Let us surrender to the lord wholeheartedly.
When we know that we will reap what we sow
Then why do anything that is undesirable?
We need to be farsighted so that we avoid sins
And we pattern our lives to win in the divine court.
So that we earn a place in it.

Salok Mahalla 1
Chaakar lagey chaakri naley garab vaad.
Gala kare ghaneria khasam na paye saad.
Aap gavaye sewa kare ta kichh paye maan.
Nanak jisno laga tis miley laga so parvan. 1

Mahalla 2
Jo jee hoi so ugavey muh ka kahiya vao.
Beejey bikh mangey amrit vekho eh niyao. 2

Mahalla 2
Naal iyaney dosti kadey na aavey raas.
Jeha jaaney teho vartey vekho ko nirjaas.
Vastu andar vast samavey duji hovey paas.
Sahib seti hukam na chaley kahi baney ardaas.
Koorh kamaney koorho hovey Nanak sifat vigaas. 3

Salok Mahalla 1
If the servant serves with pride
He is only doing lip-service
He will not gain the master's favour.
Only if he can surrender completely
He will gain something in return.
Only such a person can win the divine favour.

Mahalla 2
Whatever is in our heart is known through our expression
We don't need to articulate it
We sow poison and expect nectar in return
How fair is this?

Mahalla 2
We will gain nothing by following the foolish mind
It will give only that which it possesses.
The True One will find place in it
Only if it is emptied of all else.
We cannot demand anything from the lord.
We will get when we dissolve ourselves.
All other actions are false.

Mahalla 2
Naal iyaney dosti vadaru sio nehu.
Pani andar leek jio jis da thao na thehu. 4

Mahalla 2
Hoi iyana kare kamm aan na sakey raas.
Je ik adh changi kare duji bhi veraas. 5

Pauri
Chaakar lagey chaakri je chaley khasamey bhaye.
Hurmat tis no agli oh vajuh bhi duna khaye.
Khasamey kare barabari phir gairat andar paye.
Vajuh gavaye agla muhe muh pana khaye.
Jis da dita khavna tis kahiye sabaas.
Nanak hukam na chalyee naal khasam chaley ardaas. // 22 //

Mahalla 2
Living by the dictates of the mind is a mistake
It is like following a line in water
It is there for a moment and then is gone forever.

Mahalla 2
He who follows the mind will get nowhere
He might do one odd thing right but no more

Pauri
True service lies in accepting the divine will.
It gains respect here and hereafter.
He who tries to compete with the master
He loses everything and is punished.
We must remember the divine every moment
Without that we are as good as nothing.
We cannot demand things from Him
We can only pray to Him.

Salok Mahalla 1
Eh kinehi daat aapas te jo payeeye.
Nanak sa karmaat sahib tuthey jo miley. 1

Mahalla 2
Eh kinehi chaakri jit bhau khasam na jaye.
Nanak sewak kadiye je seti khasam samaye. 2

Pauri
Nanak ant na japni hari ta ke parawar.
Aap karaye sakhti phir aap karaye maar.
Ikna gali janjeeriya ik turi charhey bisiyar.
Aap karaye kare aap hau kei sio kari pukar.
Nanak karna jin kiya phir tis hi karni saar. // 23 //

Salok Mahalla 2
What kind of blessing is this that we can get on our own?
Blessings are those that come from His favour.

Mahalla 2
What kind of service is this which does not respect the master?
True service is that which dissolves the servant completely.

Pauri
We don't know the extent of your divine will
You make us sin and deserve punishment.
You put some of us in chains
While you let others free to fly.
You are the doer and you are the result.
You are the creator and you are the sustainer.

Salok Mahalla 1
Aape bhandey sajiyan aape puran dei.
Ikni dudh samayeeye ik chuley rahan charhey.
Ik nihali pai sawan ik upar rahan kharhey.
Tina sawarey Nanaka jin ko nadar karey.

Mahalla 2
Aape sajey kare aap jayee bhi rakhey aap.
Tis vich jant upaye kei dekhey thap uthap.
Kisno kahiye Nanaka sabh kichh aape aap. 2

Pauri
Vadey kiya vadiyayeeya kichh kahna kahan na jaye.
So karta kadar kareem de jeeya rijak sambaye.
Saayee kaar kamavni dhur chhodi tiney jaye.
Nanak eki bahri hor duji nahi jaye.
So kare je tisey rajaye. // 24 //

Salok Mahalla 1
You make the pots and you put food in them
You fill some with joys and others with sorrow.
Some of us are tense while others are carefree.
Fortunate are those that are blessed by you.

Mahalla 2
You are continuously creating and destroying
You create living beings and watch over them.
Nanak says: You are everything and everywhere.

Pauri
I have no words to praise the True One
You are the creator of nature and merciful
You provide food for each one of your creatures.
They act according to their nature
Nanak says: There is no one else except Thee
Everyone else is merely acting out Thy Will.

Salok Mahalla Naunva

Gunn Gobind gaayo nahin
Janam akarath keen
Kaho Nanak Har bhaj mana
Jeh bidh jal ko meen./1/

Bikhyan sio kahe rachiyo
Nimakh na hoye udhas.
Kaho Nanak Har bhaj mana
Parey na jamm ki phas./2/

Tarnapo eiyun hee gayo
Liyo jara tann jeet.
Kaho Nanak Har bhaj mana
Audh jaat hai beet./3/

Biradh bhaye sujhey nahin
Kaal pahunchiyo aan.
Kaho Nanak nar bavarey
Kyun na bhajey bhagwan./4/

Dhan dara sampat sagal
Jin apni kar jaan.
In mein kuchh sangi nahin
Nanak saachi maan./5/

Patit udharan bhay haran
Har anath ke nath.
Kaho Nanak teh jaaniye
Sada basat tum saath./6/

You have wasted your life
Without singing the praise of God
Nanak says remember Him now
Like the fish remembers water.

You lost yourself in worldly affairs
And never looked within for a moment
Nanak says remember Him now
Lest the noose tightens round your neck.

You have wasted your youth
Now old age sits at your doorstep
Nanak says remember Him now
The span of life is coming to an end.

Old age failed to make you realise
Now Death knocks at your door.
Nanak says: You crazy fool
Why not remember Him now?

Wealth, woman and all the riches
Which you considered your own
None of it will abide by you
Nanak says: Know this to be the truth.

He uplifts the sinners and allays fear
He is the help of the helpless
Nanak says: Know Him
Who abides by thee always.

Tan dhan jeh tau ko diyo
Ta seo neho na keen
Kaho Nanak nar bavarey
Ab kiyun dolat deen./7/

Tan dhan sampeh sukh diyo
Ar jeh neekey dham
Kaho Nanak sunn re mana
Simrat kahey na Ram./8/

Sab sukh daata Ram hai
Doosar nahi na koye
Kaho Nanak sunn re manna
Teh simrat gati hoye./9/

Jeh simrat gati paayiye
Teh bhaj re tai meet
Kaho Nanak sunn re manna
Audh ghatat hai neet./10/

Paanch tatt ko tan rachiyo
Jaanho chatur sujaan.
Jeh tey upajayio Nanaka
Leen tahey mein maan./11/

Ghat ghat menh harju baseh
Santan kaheyo pukar.
Kaho Nanak teh bhaj mana
Bhaunidh uttarey paar./12/

You didn't spare an emotion for Him
Who gave you your body and wealth.
Nanak says: You crazy fool
Now why are you reeling in fear?

He who gave you your body and wealth
And all the joys for body and soul.
Nanak says: Listen to me my mind
Why don't you remember Ram?

Ram is the bestower of all joys
There is none other than Him
Nanak says: Listen to me my mind
Remembering Him you will be liberated.

He whose remembrance liberates
My friend remember Him always
Nanak says: Listen to me my mind
Your life is lessening every day.

The body is created from five elements
And it assumes to be very intelligent.
Nanak says: The creation of five elements
Returns to its source and is absorbed.

The Lord resides in every heart
The saints have shouted from the rooftops
Nanak says: My mind remember Him
So that you cross the ocean of this world.

176

Sukh dukh jeh parsey nahin
Lobh moh abhiman.
Kaho Nanak sunn re mana
So murat bhagwan./13/

Ustat nindya nahin jeh
Kanchan loh samaan
Kaho Nanak sunn re mana
Mukat tahe tai jaan./14/

Harakh sog jaakey nahin
Bairi meet samaan.
Kaho Nanak sunn re mana
Mukat tahe tai jaan./15/

Bhai kahu dait nahi
Nahi bhai maanat aan.
Kaho Nanak sunn re mana
Gyani tahe bakhaan./16/

Jeh bikhya sagli taji
Liyo bhekh bairag.
Kaho Nanak sunn re mana
Teh nar mathey bhaag./17/

Jeh maya mamta taji
Sab te bhayio udhas
Kaho Nanak sunn re mana
Teh ghat Brahm niwas./18/

He who is not touched by joys or sorrows
As well as greed, attachments and pride.
Nanak says: Listen to me my mind
That is the form of God

He who is unaffected by praise or calumny
And for whom gold and iron are the same
Nanak says: Listen to me my mind
Such a man is liberated.

He who considers joys and sorrows alike
And to whom friend and foe are the same.
Nanak says: Listen to me my mind
Such a man is liberated.

He who does not frighten others
And is fearless of them.
Nanak says: Listen to me my mind
That is the definition of a wise man.

He who has renounced all falsehood
And has adopted the mantle of a recluse
Nanak says: Listen to me my mind
He has the mark of fortune on his brow.

He who has penetrated the appearances
And has dived into the reality.
Nanak says: Listen to me my mind
God resides in the heart of such a man.

Jeh prani haumai taji
Karta Ram pachhaan.
Kaho Nanak voh mukat nar
Eh mann saachi jaan./19/

Bhai naasan durmat haran
Kali meh Har ko naam.
Nisidin jo Nanak bhajeh
Safal hohe tai kaam./20/

Jehba gunn Gobind bhajoh
Karan sunno Har naam.
Kaho Nanak sunn re mana
Pareh na jamm ke dham./21/

Jo prani mamata tajey
Lobh moh ahankaar.
Kaho Nanak aapan tarey
Auran laet udhaar./22/

Jion supna aur pekhna
Aise jag ko jaan.
In meh kachh saacho nahin
Nanak bin bhagwan./23/

Nisidin maya karaney
Prani dolat neet.
Kotan meh Nanak koyu
Narain jeh cheet./24/

The man who has transcended his ego
And has encountered Ram.
Nanak says that man is free
There is no doubt in it.

The only destroyer of fear and wickedness
In Kaliyug is the Naam of Hari.
Nanak says remembering Him day and night
Is enough to lead a fruitful life.

Let the tongue articulate praise of Gobind
And allow the ears to hear the Naam of Hari
Nanak says: Listen to me my mind
You will not fall into the trap of death.

He who elevates himself from attachments,
Greed, ignorance and pride.
Nanak says he will ferry across himself
And will take others on his tide.

As you view the scenes in a dream
View the world in the same manner.
There is not a trace of truth in it
Says Nanak, without the divine light.

Day in and day out, man sways
For the sake of maya.
Nanak says out of millions only one
Perhaps will let Narain dwell in his heart.

Jaise jal te budbuda
Upajey binsey neet
Jag rachna taisey rachi
Kaho Nanak sunn meet./25/

Prani kachhu na chetayee
Madhu maya ke andh.
Kaho Nanak bin Har bhajan
Parat tahe jamm phandh./26/

Jo sukh ko chahe sada
Saran Ram ki leh
Kaho Nanak sunn re mana
Durlabh manukh deh./27/

Maya kaaran dhavahi
Murakh log ajaan.
Kaho Nanak bin Har bhajan
Birtha janam siraan./28/

Jo prani nisidin bhajey
Roop Ram teh jaan.
Harjan Har antar nahin
Nanak saachi maan./29/

Mann maya meh phadh rahiyo
Bisriyo Gobind naam
Kaho Nanak bin Har bhajan
Jeevan kauney kaam./30/

Like bubbles in the water
Rise and fall all day.
Such is the nature of the world
Nanak says: Know that my friend.

Man does not remember Him
Deluded by the allures of maya.
Nanak says without the anchor of Hari
He is bound to get caught by death.

If you desire peace and happiness
Come to the shelter of Ram.
Nanak says: Listen carefully
Your only opportunity is the human form.

The foolish and the ignorant people
Chase the shadows of maya endlessly.
Nanak says: Without the Naam of Hari
Your birth has been a total waste.

He who remembers Him day and night
Is the incarnation of God.
God's men and God are not different
Nanak says: Know this to be the truth.

The mind is deeply involved in maya
And has forgotten the Naam of Gobind
Nanak says: Without the song of Hari
What is the worth of this life?

Prani Ram na chetayee
Madhu maya ke andh
Kaho Nanak Har bhajan bin
Parat tahe jamm phandh./31/

Sukh mein bahu sangi bhaye
Dukh mein sang na koi.
Kaho Nanak Har bhaj mana
Ant sahayee hoi./32/

Janam janam bharmat phiriyo
Mitiyo na jamm ko traas.
Kaho Nanak Har bhaj mana
Nirbhai paaveh baas./33/

Jatan bahut main kar rahiyo
Mitiyo na mann ko maan.
Durmat sio Nanak phadiyo
Raakh leyo bhagwan./34/

Bal juwani ar biradh phun
Teen awastha jaan.
Kaho Nanak Har bhajan bin
Birtha sabh hee jaan./35/

Karano ho to so na kiyo
Pariyo lobh ke phandh.
Nanak samayo ramm gayo
Ab kiyun rovat andh./36/

Deluded by the snares of maya
Man does not remember Ram.
Nanak says: Without the song of Hari
The noose will tighten round his neck.

There are many friends of fair weather
But no one stays with you in adversity.
Nanak says: Remember Him, my mind
Who will be there for you in the end.

You have gone through many lives
Still the fear of death hangs over you.
Nanak says: Remember Him, my mind
So that you may live fearlessly.

I have tried many methods
But have failed to dissolve the ego.
Nanak is caught in the trap of evil
O Lord! Save me!

Childhood, youth and old age
These are the three stages of life
Nanak says: Without the song of Hari
All of them are sheer waste.

When there was still time you lost it
Absorbed in the labyrinths of greed.
Nanak says: Time has slipped out of hand
Now why do you cry over spilt milk?

Mann maya meh ramm rahiyo
Niksat nahin na meet.
Nanak murat chitar jion
Chhadat nahin na bheet./37/

Nar chahat kachh aur
Aurey ki aurey bhayee.
Chitwat rahiyo thagor
Nanak phansi gal paree./38/

Jatan bahut sukh ke keeyey
Dukh ko kiyo na koi.
Kaho Nanak sunn re mana
Har bhavey so hoi./39/

Jagat bhikhari phirat hai
Sabh ko daata Ram.
Kaho Nanak mann simrat teh
Puran hoveh kaam./40/

Jhoothey maan kaha karey
Jag supne jion jaan.
In meh kachhu tero nahin
Nanak kahiyo bakhaan./41/

Garab karat hai deh ko
Binsey chhinn meh meet.
Jeh prani Har jas kahiyo
Nanak teh jag jeet./42/

The mind is drowned in maya
And finds it difficult to come out of it.
Nanak says: Like the picture caught
In its frame cannot leave its cage.

Man proposes something
But something quite different happens.
Nanak says: While he is robbed by maya
The rope round his neck tightens.

I made many efforts to attain happiness
But not once did I plan for unhappiness.
Nanak says: Listen to me my mind
Only His Will prevails.

The entire world is a beggar
The only giver is Ram.
Nanak says: Remember Him
And all will be done.

What makes you feel false pride?
Know that the world is made of dream stuff.
Nanak says loud and clear
Know that nothing in it belongs to you.

You are proud of your body
It will disintegrate in a second.
Nanak says: Only the man who sings
The song of Hari, wins in the end.

Jeh ghat simran Ram ko
So nar mukta jaan.
Teh nar Har antar nahin
Nanak saachi maan./43/

Ek bhagat bhagwan jeh
Prani keh nahin mann.
Jaise sookar suwan
Nanak mano tahey tann./44/

Swami ko greh jion sada
Suwan tajat nahi nit.
Nanak ih bidh Har bhajoh
Ik mann hoi ik chit./45/

Teerath barat aur daan kar
Mann meh dharey ghumaan.
Nanak nehfal jaat hai
Jion kunchar isnaan./46/

Sir kampayo pag dagmagey
Nain jot te heen.
Kaho Nanak eh bidh bhayee
Tau na Har ras leen./47/

Nij kar dekhiyo jagat meh
Ko kahu ko nahen.
Nanak thir Har bhagat hai
Teh raakho mann mahen./48/

He whose heart beats with His remembrance
Is the only liberated person
Nanak says: There is no difference
In such a man and the Creator.

The man whose heart does not throb
With the love and devotion of God.
Nanak says: There is no difference
Between him and a pig or a dog.

Just as a dog guards his masters house
And does not leave it even for a moment.
Nanak says: Remember Him thus
With single-minded devotion.

If by visiting holy places, giving donations
And fasting the ego is strengthened.
Nanak says then all of them will go waste
Like the frog having a bath again and again.

The head is not steady, the legs tremble,
And eyes have lost their sight.
Nanak says such a state has reached
Still you do not relish the song of Hari.

I have known from personal experience
Nobody stands by any one.
Nanak says: The only anchor is Hari
Fill your heart with devotion to Him.

Jag rachna sab jhooth hai
Jaan leyo re meet.
Kahe Nanak thir na rahey
Jion balu ki bheet./49/

Ram gayo Ravan gayo
Jako bahu parivar.
Kaho Nanak thir kachhu nahin
Supne jion sansar./50/

Chinta taki keejiye
Jo anhoni hoi.
Eh marag sansar meh
Nanak thir nahin koi./51/

Jo upajiyo so binas hai
Paro aaj ke kaal.
Nanak Har gunn gaaye lai
Chhaad sagal janjaal./52/

Dohra

Bal chhutkiyo bandhan parey
Kachhu na hot upaye.
Kaho Nanak ab oat Har
Gajj jion hohey sahai./53/

Bal hoaa bandhan chhutey
Sab kichh hot upaaye.
Nanak sab kichh tumre haath meh
Tum hi hot sahaye./54/

The creation of this world is illusory
Know this fact, my friend.
Nanak says it cannot stay
And crumbles like a wall of sand.

Ram has gone and so has Ravan
And so have all their kith and kin.
Nanak says there is nothing permanent
In the world made of dream stuff.

Worry if you must
About an unnatural event.
Nanak says: On the path of this world
There is nothing permanent.

All that is born must die
Whether it is today or tomorrow.
Nanak says: Sing the song of Hari
And forget about the whole rigmarole.

Dohra

Strength wanes and chains bind me
I cannot see a way out.
Nanak says: At such a time
Hari will support you like an elephant.

Strength has returned to me and chains have
Broken, showing me all the remedies.
Nanak says: Everything is in His Hand
He will come for your help always.

Sang sakha sab tajj gaye
Kou na nibhayo saath.
Kaho Nanak eh bipat meh
Tek ek Raghunath./55/

Naam rahiyo sadhu rahiyo
Rahiyo Gur Gobind.
Kaho Nanak eh jagat meh
Kin japiyo gur mant./56/

Ram naam ur meh gahiyo
Jake samm nahin koi.
Jeh simrat sankat mitey
Daras tuharo hoi./57/

All friends and dear ones have left you
No one can be with you till the end.
Nanak says: In this time of reckoning
Only Raghunath will be with you.

Naam stays and saints stay
And stays Gur Gobind.
Nanak says: Only they stay in this world
Who remember the Guru's mantra.

Hold the name of Ram in your heart
There is nothing like it anywhere.
It allays all problems and difficulties
And helps you encounter Him.

294.682